Glencoe Science

BIOLOGY

The Dynamics of Life

Unit 3 Resources
The Life of a Cell

 **Glencoe**

New York, New York   Columbus, Ohio   Chicago, Illinois   Peoria, Illinois   Woodland Hills, California

A GLENCOE PROGRAM

BIOLOGY: THE DYNAMICS OF LIFE

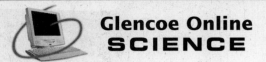

Glencoe Online
SCIENCE

Visit the Glencoe Science Web site
bdol.glencoe.com

You'll find:

Standardized Test Practice, Interactive Tutor, Section and Chapter Self-Check Quizzes, Online Student Edition, Web Links, Microscopy Links, WebQuest Projects, Internet BioLabs, In the News, Textbook Updates, Teacher Bulletin Board, Teaching Today

and much more!

The **McGraw·Hill** Companies

Send all inquiries to:
Glencoe/McGraw-Hill
8787 Orion Place
Columbus, OH 43240-4027

ISBN 0-07-860214-9

Printed in the United States of America.

3 4 5 6 7 8 9 10   009   08 07 06 05

Contents

To the Teacher

This unit-based booklet contains resource materials to help you teach this unit more effectively. You will find in chapter order:

Reproducible Pages

Hands-on Activities

MiniLab and BioLab Worksheets: Each activity in this book is an expanded version of each BioLab or MiniLab that appears in the Student Edition of *Biology: The Dynamics of Life*. All materials lists, procedures, and questions are repeated so that students can read and complete a lab in most cases without having a textbook on the lab table. Data tables are enlarged so that students can record data in them. All lab questions are reprinted with lines on which students can write their answers. In addition, for student safety, all appropriate safety symbols and caution statements have been reproduced on these expanded pages. Answer pages for each MiniLab and BioLab are included in the Teacher Support and Planning section at the back of this book.

Real World BioApplications: These two-page activities provide students with the opportunity to explore a technological or everyday application of biology. Each activity is directly related to a major concept in the Student Edition, and several examine principles from the physical sciences that underlie the biology content. While some activities are more hands-on, all require critical thinking and creativity. The teaching notes in the Teacher Support and Planning section at the back of this book suggest chapters and topics with which to correlate the activities, explain the purpose of each activity, offer materials tips and teaching strategies, and provide answers to all questions on the student pages.

Extension and Intervention

Reinforcement and Study Guide in English and Spanish: These pages help students understand, organize, and compare the main biology concepts in the textbook. The questions and activities also help build strong study and reading skills. There are four study guide pages for each chapter and two pages for the BioDigest. Students will find these pages easy to follow because the section titles match those in the textbook. Italicized sentences in the study guide direct students to the related topics in the text.

The *Reinforcement and Study Guide* exercises employ a variety of formats including short-answer questions, multiple-choice, matching, true/false, ordering, labeling, completion, and short essay. The clear, easy-to-follow exercises and the self-pacing format are geared to build your students' confidence in understanding biology. The English pages are followed immediately by the study guide pages in Spanish.

Concept Mapping: The *Concept Mapping* worksheets reinforce and extend the graphic organizational skills introduced in the Skill Handbook in the Student Edition of *Biology: The Dynamics of Life*. Concept maps are visual representations of relationships among particular concepts. By using these worksheets, students will gain experience with three different types of concept maps: the *network tree*, which shows causal information, group hierarchies, and branching procedures; the *events chain*, which describes the stages of a process, the steps in a linear procedure, or a sequence of events; and the *cycle map*, which shows how a series of events interacts to produce a set of results again and again.

There is one *Concept Mapping* worksheet for each chapter in the Student Edition. Each worksheet is geared toward a specific section or sections in the chapter so that you can assign it at the most relevant time. An entire section may be mapped or just a few key concepts from the section. Answers to all *Concept Mapping* worksheets are provided in the Teacher Support and Planning section at the back of this book.

Critical Thinking/Problem Solving: For each chapter of *Biology: The Dynamics of Life,* a one-page *Critical Thinking* or *Problem Solving* worksheet is provided to extend the material in the Student Edition. Each worksheet is geared to a specific section or sections in the chapter so that you can assign it at the most relevant time. Answers to all worksheets are provided in the Teacher Support and Planning section at the back of this book.

The worksheets follow Bloom's taxonomy of problem solving. Each worksheet tests the students' abilities on one or more of the following areas:

- to use knowledge
- to comprehend what that knowledge means
- to apply that knowledge to a new but related situation
- to analyze the different aspects of new information
- to synthesize new information in order to respond to a particular situation in a creative and logical way

Transparency Activity Masters

Section Focus Transparencies: A *Section Focus Transparency* is provided for every section in the Student Edition. Each transparency contains two questions related to the transparency image. In addition, each transparency is reproduced as a master in this book. These masters are designed to generate interest and focus students' attention on the topic being presented in that section. Teaching strategies background information, and possible answers to the questions for each transparency in this unit can be found in the Teacher Support and Planning section at the back of this book.

Basic Concepts Transparencies: This book contains a blackline master version of each color *Basic Concepts Transparency* for this unit. In most cases, the transparency illustration is different than the illustration in the textbook, providing optimum support for your visual learners. The accompanying worksheet for each transparency master focuses students' attention on the topic, requiring them to analyze the illustration and relate it to the concepts being taught in the textbook. The use of the masters makes the worksheets convenient homework assignments.

Teaching strategies as well as worksheet answers are provided for each transparency. Several transparencies utilize overlays for maximum teaching benefit, and explanations of how to use these overlays are included in the teaching suggestions in the Teacher Support and Planning section at the back of this book.

Reteaching Skills Transparencies: This book contains a blackline master version of each color *Reteaching Skills Transparency* for this unit. The transparencies and masters provide visual tools for reteaching important concepts. To make your reteaching more powerful, the transparencies and masters are developed around basic skills. These skills include, but are not limited to, interpreting scientific illustrations, sequencing, recognizing cause and effect, comparing and contrasting, observing and inferring, and classifying.

The accompanying worksheet for each transparency master focuses students' attention on the topic skill. Students may find it helpful to take notes on the master and use it as a study tool for the chapter. Teaching strategies as well as worksheet answers are provided for each transparency. Several transparencies utilize overlays for maximum teaching benefit, and explanations of how to use these overlays are included in the teaching suggestions in the Teacher Support and Planning section at the back of this book.

Assessment

Chapter Assessment: These worksheets provide materials to assess your students' understanding of concepts from each chapter in this unit. Each chapter test includes several sections that assess students' understanding at different levels.

The *Reviewing Vocabulary* section tests students' knowledge of the chapter's vocabulary. A variety of formats is used, including matching, multiple-choice, and completion.

The *Understanding Main Ideas* section consists of two parts. Part A tests recall and basic understanding of facts presented in the chapter. Part B is designed to be more challenging and requires deeper comprehension of concepts than does Part A. Students may be asked to explain biological processes and relationships or to make comparisons and generalizations.

The *Thinking Critically* section requires students to use several high-order learning skills. For some questions, students will need to interpret data and discover relationships presented in graphs and tables. Other questions may require them to apply their understanding of concepts to solve problems, to compare and contrast situations, and to make inferences or predictions.

In the final section, *Applying Scientific Methods*, students are put into the role of researcher. They may be asked to read about an experiment, simulation, or model, and then apply their understanding of chapter concepts and scientific methods to analyze and explain the procedure and results. Many of the questions in this section are open-ended, giving students the opportunity to demonstrate both reasoning and creative skills. This section, as well as the other sections of each test, begins on a separate page, so that if you wish to omit a section from a test, you can easily do so.

Answers or possible responses to all questions for the chapters in this unit are provided in the Teacher Support and Planning section at the back of this book.

Student Recording Sheet: *Student Recording Sheets* allow students to use the Chapter Assessments in the Student Edition as a practice for standardized testing, giving them an opportunity to use bubble answer grids and number grids for recording answers. There is a recording sheet for each chapter in this unit and a recording sheet for the Unit Assessment at the end of the BioDigest for this unit. Answers for the *Student Recording Sheets* can be found in the side wrap of the Teacher Wraparound Edition on the Chapter Assessment and Unit Review pages.

Teacher Support and Planning

Foldables™ Study Organizer: These pages provide an additional Foldables strategy for each chapter in this unit. The strategy is presented at the top of the page along with more challenging options or suggestions for students who prefer their Foldables to be more creative or informative. The bottom of the page provides instructions for how to make Foldables and can be reproduced and distributed to students who may benefit from the illustrated instructions.

Teacher Guide and Answers: Answers or possible answers for questions in this booklet can be found in chapter order in this section. Materials, teaching strategies, and content background along with chapter references are found where appropriate.

Contents

Chapter 6

Chapter 6 The Chemistry of Life

MiniLab 6.1

Experimenting

Determine pH

The pH of a solution is a measurement of how acidic or basic that solution is. An easy way to measure the pH of a solution is to use pH paper.

Procedure

1. Pour a small amount (about 5 mL) of each of the following into separate clean, small beakers or other small glass containers: lemon juice, prepared household ammonia solution, liquid detergent, shampoo, and vinegar.
2. Dip a fresh strip of pH paper briefly into each solution and remove.
3. Compare the color of the wet paper with the pH color chart; record the pH of each material. **CAUTION:** *Wash your hands after handling lab materials.*

Analysis

1. Which solutions are acids?

_____

_____

2. Which solutions are bases?

_____

_____

3. What ions in the solution caused the pH paper to change? Which solution contained the highest concentration of hydroxide ions? How do you know?

_____

_____

MiniLab 6.2

Apply Concepts

Investigate the Rate of Diffusion

In this lab, you will place a small potato cube in a solution of purple dye and observe how far the dark purple color diffuses into the potato after a given length of time.

Procedure

1. Using a single-edge razor blade, cut a cube 1 cm on each side from a raw, peeled potato. **CAUTION:** *Be careful with sharp objects. Do not cut objects while holding them in your hand.*

2. Use forceps to carefully place the cube in a cup or beaker containing the purple solution. The solution should cover the cube. Note and record the time. Let the cube stand in the solution for between 10 and 30 minutes.

3. Using forceps, remove the cube from the solution and note the time. Cut the cube in half.

4. Measure, in millimeters, how far the purple solution has diffused, and divide this number by the time you allowed your potato to remain in the solution. This is the diffusion rate.

Analysis

1. How far did the purple solution diffuse?

_____

_____

2. What was the rate of diffusion per minute?

_____

_____

Does temperature affect an enzyme reaction?

Chapter **6**

Problem

Does the enzyme peroxidase work in cold temperatures? Does peroxidase work better at higher temperatures? Does peroxidase work after being frozen or boiled?

Hypotheses

Make a hypothesis regarding how you think temperature will affect the rate at which the enzyme peroxidase breaks down hydrogen peroxide. Consider both low and high temperatures.

Objectives

In this BioLab, you will:
- **Observe** the activity of an enzyme.
- **Compare** the activity of the enzyme at various temperatures.

Possible Materials

clock or timer   ice
400-mL beaker   hot plate
kitchen knife   waxed paper
tongs or large forceps   thermometer
5-mm thick potato slices
3% hydrogen peroxide

Safety Precautions

Be sure to wash your hands before and after handling the lab materials. Always wear goggles in the lab.

Skill Handbook

Use the **Skill Handbook** if you need additional help with this lab.

PLAN THE EXPERIMENT

1. Decide on a way to test your group's hypothesis. Keep the available materials in mind.
2. When testing the activity of the enzyme at a certain temperature, consider the length of time it will take for the potato to reach that temperature, and how the temperature will be measured.
3. To test for peroxidase activity, add 1 drop of hydrogen peroxide to the potato slice and observe what happens.
4. When heating a thin potato slice, first place it in a small amount of water in a beaker. Then heat the beaker slowly so that the temperature of the water and the temperature of the slice are always the same. Try to make observations at several temperatures between 10°C and 100°C.

Check the Plan

Discuss the following points with other groups to decide on the final procedure for your experiment.

1. What data will you collect? How will you record them?
2. What factors should be controlled?
3. What temperatures will you test?
4. How will you achieve those temperatures?
5. *Make sure your teacher has approved your experimental plan before you proceed further.*
6. Carry out your experiment. **CAUTION:** *Be careful with chemicals and heat. Hydrogen peroxide is a skin and eye irritant. Wash your hands after the lab.*
7. **Cleanup and Disposal** Follow your teacher's instructions.

Does temperature affect an enzyme reaction?, *continued*

ANALYZE AND CONCLUDE

1. Identify Effects Describe your observations of the effects of peroxidase on hydrogen peroxide.

_____

_____

_____

_____

2. Checking Your Hypothesis Do your data support or reject your hypothesis? Explain your results.

_____

_____

_____

_____

3. Analyzing Data At what temperature did peroxidase work best?

_____

4. Recognizing Cause and Effect If you've ever used hydrogen peroxide as an antiseptic to treat a cut or scrape, you know that it foams as soon as it touches an open wound. How can you account for this observation?

_____

_____

_____

_____

5. Error Analysis What factors did you need to control in your tests? What might have caused errors in your results?

_____

_____

_____

_____

6 How Lean Is Lean Ground Beef?

Nutritionists caution against diets that include too much fat. However, the body needs some fat. Fats are one of the six essential nutrients, are a major energy source for the body, and are important building blocks of cell membranes. To lower your intake of dietary fats, nutritionists suggest that you avoid junk food, cut down on dairy products, and eat leaner meats such as chicken or lean ground beef. Supermarkets offer consumers different types of lean ground beef, such as 75 percent lean, 85 percent lean, and 95 percent lean. But are these lean varieties of beef really worth the added cost, and are they really as lean as advertised? In this activity, you'll answer these questions as you determine the fat content in three samples of ground beef.

PROCEDURE

1. Obtain and label three different samples of ground beef, and record information about each sample in Table 1. Calculate the beef's cost per 100 grams by dividing the price per pound by 454 and multiplying by 100.

Table 1

Ground Beef Sample	Percentage of Fat on Label	Cost per 100 Grams
1		
2		
3		

2. Using a balance, weigh out a 100-g sample of ground beef and place it in a large beaker labeled Sample 1. Fill the beaker three-fourths full with water, set it on a hot plate, and heat to boiling. **CAUTION:** *Use care when working with a heat source.*

3. Use tongs or gloves to remove the beaker from the heat source, and allow it to cool 10 minutes.

4. The fat will form a separate layer above the water. Pour as much of the fat as you can into a graduated cylinder. Use care so as not to pour off water into the graduated cylinder. It may be necessary to gently scrape remaining fat particles from the beaker and add them to the graduated cylinder. Determine the volume of fat in ground beef Sample 1, and record this in Table 2. Calculate the mass of the fat by multiplying the volume of fat by 0.9 gm/mL, the density of fat.

5. Calculate the percentage of fat by dividing the mass of fat by the mass of Sample 1 and multiplying by 100%. Record the percentage of fat in Table 2.

6. Repeat steps 2 through 5 for the other two beef samples.

Real World BioApplications

Table 2

Ground Beef Sample	Mass (g)	Volume of Fat (mL)	Mass of Fat (g)	Percentage of Fat in Sample
1				
2				
3				

ANALYZE AND CONCLUDE

1. Which ground beef sample had the lowest percentage of fat? The highest?

_____

_____

2. Do your experimental percentages of fat agree with those stated on the labels of the ground beef samples? What might account for differences between the values?

_____

_____

_____

_____

3. Which of the ground beef samples would you be most likely to buy? Explain your answer.

_____

_____

_____

Chapter 6 The Chemistry of Life

Reinforcement and Study Guide

Section 6.1 Atoms and Their Interactions

In your textbook, read about elements, atoms, and isotopes.

If the statement is true, write *true*. If it is not, rewrite the italicized part to make it true.

1. An element is a substance that *can be* broken down into simpler substances. _____

2. On Earth, *about 25* elements are essential to living organisms. _____

3. Only four elements—*carbon, hydrogen, oxygen, and nitrogen*—make up more than 96 percent of the mass of a human. _____

4. Each element is abbreviated by a one- or two-letter *formula*. _____

5. Trace elements, such as iron and magnesium, are present in living things in *very large* amounts. _____

6. The properties of elements are determined by *the structures of their atoms*. _____

Label the parts of the atom. Use these choices:

energy level   electron   neutron   proton   nucleus

11. _____

7. _____

10. _____

8. _____

9. _____

Answer the following questions.

12. What is the maximum number of electrons in each of the following energy levels: first, second, third? _____

13. Boron has two isotopes, boron-10 and boron-11. Boron-10 has five protons and five neutrons. How many protons and neutrons does boron-11 have? Explain. _____

Reinforcement and Study Guide

Section 6.1 Atoms and Their Interactions

In your textbook, read about compounds and bonding, chemical reactions, and mixtures and solutions.

Write the type of substance described. Use these choices: compound, element.

_____ **14.** H_2O, a liquid that no longer resembles either hydrogen or oxygen gas

_____ **15.** A substance that can be broken down in a chemical reaction

_____ **16.** Carbon, the substance represented by the symbol C

Complete the table by checking the correct column for each description.

Statement	Ionic Bond(s)	Covalent Bond(s)
17. Found in the compound NaCl		
18. Increases the stability of atoms		
19. Results in the formation of a molecule		
20. Is formed when atoms share electrons		

Fill in the blanks with the correct number of molecules to balance the chemical equation. Then answer the questions.

$$C_6H_{12}O_6 + \underline{} O_2 \longrightarrow \underline{} CO_2 + \underline{} H_2O$$

21. Why must chemical equations always balance?

_____

_____

22. Which number indicates the number of atoms of each element in a molecule of a substance.

_____

23. When is a mixture not a solution?

_____

_____

24. What is the difference between an acid and a base?

_____

_____

Chapter 6 **The Chemistry of Life,** *continued*

Section 6.2 Water and Diffusion

In your textbook, read about water and its importance.

For each statement below, write <u>true</u> or <u>false</u>.

_____ **1.** In a water molecule, electrons are shared equally between the hydrogen atoms and oxygen atom.

_____ **2.** The attraction of opposite charges between hydrogen and oxygen forms a weak oxygen bond.

_____ **3.** Because of its polarity, water can move from the roots of a plant up to its leaves.

_____ **4.** Water changes temperature easily.

_____ **5.** Unlike most substances, water expands when it freezes.

Circle the letter of the choice that best completes the statement.

6. All objects in motion have
  a. potential energy.   **b.** heat energy.   **c.** kinetic energy.   **d.** random energy.

7. The first scientist to observe evidence of the random motion of molecules was
  a. Brown.   **b.** Darwin.   **c.** Mendel.   **d.** Hooke.

8. The net movement of particles from an area of higher concentration to an area of lower concentration is called
  a. dynamic equilibrium.   **b.** nonrandom movement.
  c. concentration gradient.   **d.** diffusion.

9. Diffusion occurs because of
  a. nonrandom movement of particles.   **b.** random movement of particles.
  c. a chemical reaction between particles. **d.** chemical energy.

10. When a few drops of colored corn syrup are added to a beaker of pure corn syrup, the color will
  a. move from low concentration to high concentration.
  b. form a polar bond.
  c. start to diffuse.
  d. remain on the bottom of the beaker.

11. Diffusion can be accelerated by
  a. decreasing the pressure.   **b.** increasing the temperature.
  c. decreasing the movement of particles. **d.** increasing the dynamic equilibrium.

12. When materials pass into and out of a cell at equal rates, there is no net change in concentration inside the cell. The cell is in a state of
  a. dynamic equilibrium. **b.** metabolism.   **c.** imbalance.   **d.** inertia.

13. The difference in concentration of a substance across space is called
  a. dynamic equilibrium.   **b.** concentration gradient.
  c. diffusion.   **d.** Brownian movement.

In your textbook, read about the role of carbon in organisms.

For each of the following statements about carbon, write <u>true</u> or <u>false</u>.

_____ **1.** Carbon atoms can bond together in straight chains, branched chains, or rings.

_____ **2.** Large molecules containing carbon atoms are called micromolecules.

_____ **3.** Polymers are formed by hydrolysis.

_____ **4.** Cells use carbohydrates for energy.

Write each item below under the correct heading.

sucrose   glucose   starch $C_6H_{12}O_6$
cellulose   glycogen   fructose $C_{12}H_{22}O_{11}$

Monosaccharide	Dissaccharide	Polysaccharide
5.	8.	10.
6.	9.	11.
7.		12.

Complete the table by checking the correct column for each description.

Description	Lipids	Proteins	Nucleic Acids
13. Made up of nucleotides			
14. Most consist of three fatty acids bonded to a glycerol molecule			
15. DNA and RNA			
16. Contain peptide bonds			
17. Produce proteins			
18. Commonly called fats and oils			
19. Made up of amino acids			
20. Used for long-term energy storage, insulation, and protective coatings			
21. Contain carbon, hydrogen, oxygen, and nitrogen			

Capítulo 6 — La química de la vida

Refuerzo y Guía de estudio

Sección 6.1 Los átomos y sus interacciones

En tu libro de texto, lee acerca de los elementos, los átomos y los isótopos.

Si el enunciado es verdadero, escribe *verdadero*; de lo contrario, modifica la sección en itálicas para hacer verdadero el enunciado.

1. Un elemento es una sustancia que *puede* ser descompuesta en sustancias más simples. _____

2. Existen *unos 25* elementos esenciales para los seres vivos en la Tierra. _____

3. Más del 96 por ciento de la masa del cuerpo humano está formada por sólo cuatro elementos: *carbono, hidrógeno, oxígeno y nitrógeno*. _____

4. Los elementos se abrevian mediante una *fórmula* que consta de una o dos letras. _____

5. Los elementos traza, como el hierro y el magnesio, están presentes en los seres vivos en *grandes* cantidades. _____

6. Las propiedades de los elementos están determinadas por *la estructura de sus átomos*. _____

Identifica las partes del átomo. Usa las siguientes opciones:

nivel de energía   electrón   neutrón   protón   núcleo

7. _____
8. _____
9. _____
10. _____
11. _____

Contesta las siguientes preguntas.

12. ¿Cuál es el número máximo de electrones que pueden contener los siguientes niveles de electrones: primero, segundo y tercero?

_____

13. El boro tiene dos isótopos boro-10 y boro 11. El boro-10 tiene cinco protones y cinco neutrones. ¿Cuántos protones y neutrones tiene el boro-11? Explica.

_____

Capítulo 6 La química de la vida, *continuación*

Sección 6.1 Los átomos y sus interacciones

En tu libro de texto, lee sobre los compuestos y enlaces, las reacciones químicas, y las mezclas y soluciones.

Identifica si el tipo de sustancia descrita es un compuesto o un elemento.

_____ **14.** H_2O, líquido que ya no se parece ni al gas hidrógeno ni al gas oxígeno

_____ **15.** Una sustancia que puede ser descompuesta por una reacción química

_____ **16.** Carbono, la sustancia representada con el símbolo C

Completa la tabla indicando la columna correspondiente a cada enunciado.

Enunciado	Enlace iónico	Enlace covalente
17. Se encuentra en el compuesto NaCl		
18. Aumenta la estabilidad de los átomos		
19. Ocasiona la formación de una molécula		
20. Se forma cuando los átomos comparten electrones		

Anota en los espacios correspondientes el número de moléculas que se requieren para balancear la ecuación química. Luego, contesta las preguntas.

$$C_6H_{12}O_6 \; + \underline{} O_2 \longrightarrow \underline{} CO_2 \; + \underline{} H_2O$$

21. ¿Por qué las ecuaciones químicas siempre deben estar balanceadas?

_____

_____

22. ¿Cuál número indica el número de átomos de cada elemento en una molécula de una sustancia?

_____

23. ¿En qué ocasiones una mezcla no es una solución?

_____

_____

24. ¿Cuál es la diferencia entre un ácido y una base?

_____

_____

Capítulo 6 La química de la vida, *continuación*

En tu libro de texto, lee acerca del agua y su importancia.

Indica si cada enunciado es <u>verdadero</u> o <u>falso</u>.

_____ **1.** En la molécula de agua, los átomos de hidrógeno comparten equitativamente los electrones con el átomo de oxígeno.

_____ **2.** La atracción de cargas opuestas entre el hidrógeno y el oxígeno forma un enlace de oxígeno débil.

_____ **3.** Debido a su polaridad, el agua se puede desplazar desde las raíces hasta las hojas de las plantas.

_____ **4.** El agua cambia de temperatura fácilmente.

_____ **5.** A diferencia de muchas otras sustancias, el agua se expande cuando se congela.

Haz un círculo alrededor de la letra de la opción que completa mejor cada enunciado.

6. Todos los cuerpos en movimiento tienen
   a. energía potencial.   **b.** energía calorífica.   **c.** energía cinética.   **d.** energía aleatoria.

7. El primer científico que observó la evidencia del movimiento aleatorio de las moléculas fue
   a. Brown.   **b.** Darwin.   **c.** Mendel.   **d.** Hooke.

8. El movimiento neto de partículas desde un área de mayor concentración hacia un área de menor concentración se llama
   a. equilibrio dinámico.   **b.** movimiento no aleatorio.
   c. gradiente de concentración.   **d.** difusión.

9. La difusión ocurre debido
   a. al movimiento no aleatorio de las partículas.   **b.** al movimiento aleatorio de las partículas
   c. a la reacción química entre las partículas.   **d.** a la energía química.

10. Al añadir unas gotas de jarabe coloreado a un vaso de precipitados con jarabe puro, el colorante
   a. se desplazará desde la zona de baja concentración hacia la zona de alta concentración.
   b. formará enlaces polares.
   c. se difundirá.
   d. permanecerá en el fondo del vaso de precipitados.

11. La difusión se acelera si
   a. disminuye la presión.   **b.** aumenta la temperatura.
   c. disminuye el movimiento de las partículas.   **d.** aumenta el equilibrio dinámico.

12. Cuando los materiales entran y salen a la mima tasa de una célula, no hay un cambio neto en la concentración de materiales dentro de la célula. La célula está en un estado de
   a. equilibrio dinámico.   **b.** metabolismo.   **c.** desequilibrio.   **d.** inercia.

13. La diferencia en la concentración de una sustancia a través del espacio se llama
   a. equilibrio dinámico.   **b.** gradiente de concentración.
   c. difusión.   **d.** movimiento browniano.

En tu libro de texto, lee sobre la importancia del carbono en los organismos.

Indica si cada enunciado es <u>verdadero</u> o <u>falso</u>.

_____ **1.** Al unirse, los átomos de carbono pueden formar cadenas lineales, cadenas ramificadas o anillos.

_____ **2.** Las micromoléculas son moléculas grandes que contienen átomos de carbono.

_____ **3.** Los polímeros se forman por hidrólisis.

_____ **4.** Las células usan carbohidratos para obtener energía.

Anota cada término en la columna que le corresponde.

sacarosa   glucosa   almidón $C_6H_{12}O_6$

celulosa   glucógeno   fructosa $C_{12}H_{22}O_{11}$

Monosacárido	Disacárido	Polisacárido
5.	8.	10.
6.	9.	11.
7.		12.

Completa la tabla indicando la columna correspondiente a cada enunciado.

Descripción	Lípidos	Proteínas	Ácidos nucleicos
13. Formado por nucleótidos			
14. En general, constan de tres ácidos grasos unidos a una molécula de glicerol			
15. DNA y RNA			
16. Contienen enlaces peptídicos			
17. Produce proteínas			
18. Se conocen como grasas y aceites			
19. Formados(as) por aminoácidos			
20. Sirven para almacenar energía a largo plazo, para aislar y como protección			
21. Contienen carbono, hidrógeno, oxígeno e hidrógeno			

Chapter

6   The Chemistry of Life

Concept Mapping

Use with Chapter 6, Section 6.2

Properties of Water Important to Living Systems

Complete the concept map on the properties of water. Use these words or phrases once: *other water molecules, float in water, hydrogen bond with, resistance, thin plant tubes, temperature, be less dense, capillary action, expansion, attract, break rocks, freezes, cellular functions.*

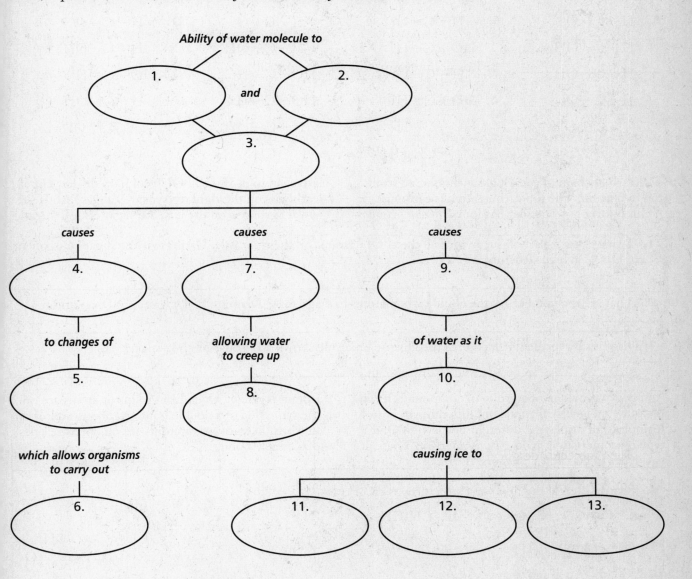

Chapter
6 **The Chemistry of Life**

Critical Thinking

Use with Chapter 6, Section 6.3

Sugars and Isomers

Sugars are common carbohydrates. They are either simple sugars (monosaccharides) or complex sugars (polysaccharides). Sugars are usually drawn as ring structures, but they are sometimes pictured as chains in order to show the positions of all atoms. Pictured below are four common sugars.

A.
H—C=O
|
H—C—OH
|
H—C—OH
|
H—C—OH
|
CH_2OH

B.
H—C=O
|
HO—C—H
|
H—C—OH
|
HO—C—H
|
HO—C—H
|
CH_2OH

C.
H—C=O
|
H—C—OH
|
HO—C—H
|
HO—C—H
|
H—C—OH
|
CH_2OH

D.
H—C=O
|
H—C—OH
|
HO—C—H
|
H—C—OH
|
CH_2OH

The carbon chain of each sugar is numbered from top to bottom. The top carbon atom is carbon 1. A chiral carbon is one that has four *different* groups attached to it. If the —OH group on the last chiral carbon is on the right, the sugar is a D-sugar. If the —OH group is on the left, the sugar is an L-sugar.

1. D-ribose is a 5-carbon sugar with all the —OH groups on the right side. D-ribose is the sugar component of DNA. Which structure is D-ribose?

_____

2. What are the numbers of the chiral carbon atoms in diagram A? Diagram B? Diagram C? Diagram D?

_____

3. Diagram B represents glucose. Is the glucose molecule shown a D-sugar or an L-sugar?

_____

An *isomer* is any one of a group of compounds having the same molecular formula but different structural formulas and displaying different properties. One type of isomerism is geometric isomerism. There are two types of geometric isomers. A *cis* isomer is one in which like groups or atoms are on the same side of a double bond. A *trans* isomer is one in which like groups or atoms are on opposite sides of a double bond.

4. Identify each of the following structures as cis or trans.

a.
CH_3 CH_3
  \   /
   C=C
  /   \
H   H

_____

b.
CH_3CH_2 H
     \   /
      C=C
     /   \
   H CH_3CH_2

_____

c.
O
‖
 C(CH_2)   H
      \   /
       C=C
      /   \
H_3C H   O
                    ‖
                    C
                    |
                    OH

_____

5. *cis*-9-Tricosine, $CH_3(CH_2)_7CH = CH(CH_2)_{12}CH_3$, is the active sex attractant in the common housefly. Draw the structure of this compound. What would be the trans isomer of 9-tricosine? Draw its structure.

Master
12 **Elements**

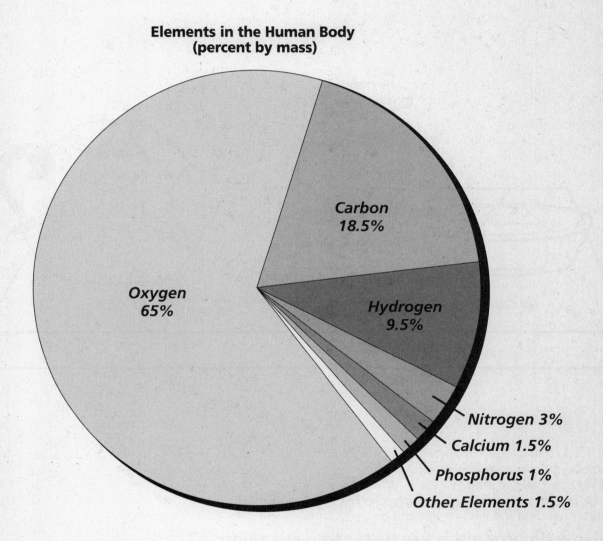

Elements in the Human Body
(percent by mass)

Oxygen
65%

Carbon
18.5%

Hydrogen
9.5%

Nitrogen 3%
Calcium 1.5%
Phosphorus 1%
Other Elements 1.5%

1 Which four elements are the most common in the human body?

2 What do you know about these four elements?

Master
13 **Water**

Use with Chapter 6, Section 6.2

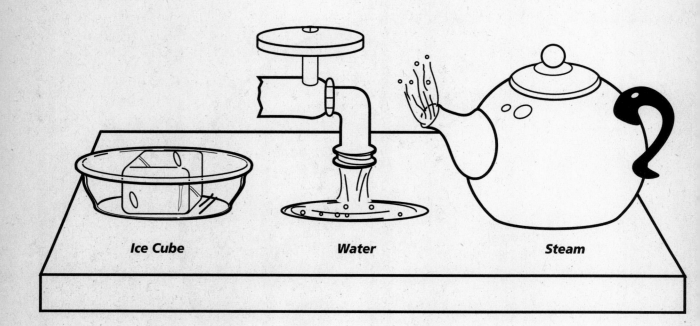

Ice Cube   Water   Steam

❶ What are some characteristics of water?

❷ How do organisms use water to live and grow?

Master 14 **Elements in Different Combinations**

❶ How many different letters are in the words? What other words can you make from these letters?

❷ Use the example to explain how only 90 natural elements could form all the different substances on Earth.

Name _____ Date _____ Class _____

Master 4

Atomic Structure

Basic Concepts

Use with Chapter 6, Section 6.1

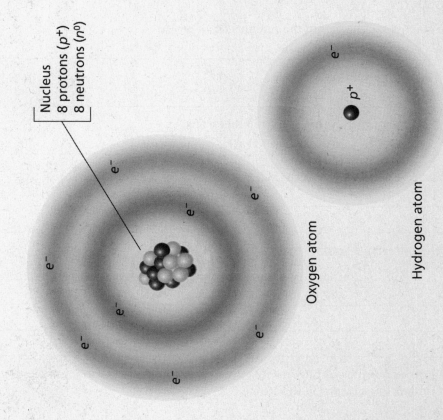

Nucleus
8 protons (p^+)
8 neutrons (n^0)

e^-

Oxygen atom

e^-

p^+

Hydrogen atom

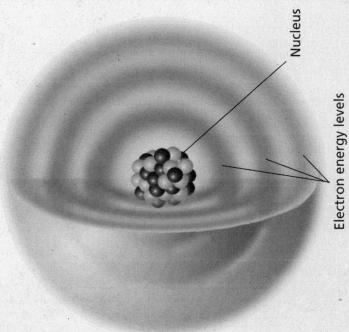

Nucleus

Electron energy levels

Worksheet 4 **Atomic Structure**

1. What atomic particles occupy the nucleus of an atom?

2. What is the charge on the nucleus?

3. Describe the location and movement of electrons.

4. Explain the difference among energy levels.

5. If you knew the number of protons in a given atom, how would that enable you to figure out the number of electrons in the atom?

6. How are the electrons arranged in an oxygen atom?

7. Why is hydrogen considered to have the simplest atomic structure?

8. What determines the characteristics of the atoms shown in the illustration?

Master 5a Covalent Bonding

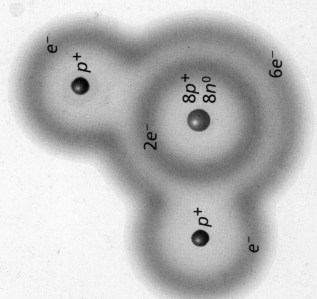

Water molecule

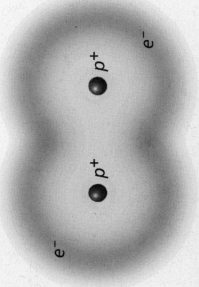

Hydrogen molecule

Master 5b   Ionic Bonding

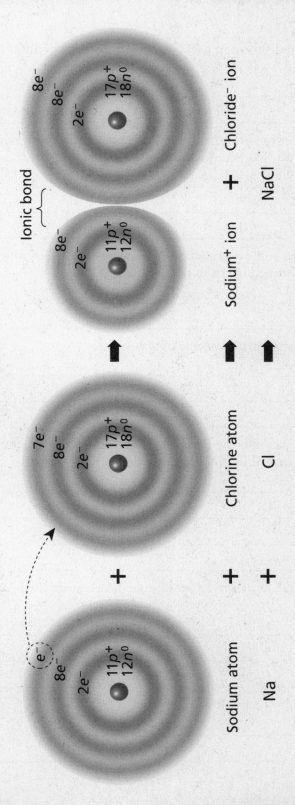

Worksheet 5 — Covalent and Ionic Bonding

1. How does the compound shown in part 5a of the transparency differ from the elements that comprise it?

   _____

   _____

2. How does a hydrogen atom differ from the other atoms shown in parts 5a and 5b of the transparency in terms of what is required for it to become stable?

   _____

   _____

3. Describe how hydrogen and oxygen atoms react with each other to form a compound. What kind of bond is formed between the atoms?

   _____

   _____

   _____

4. What is the overall charge on a molecule of water?

   _____

   _____

   _____

5. Describe how sodium and chlorine atoms react with each other to form a compound. What kind of bond is formed between the atoms?

   _____

   _____

   _____

   _____

6. Why does hydrogen exist in nature as a molecule of two atoms rather than as separate atoms?

   _____

   _____

   _____

7. What is one biological process that requires ions?

   _____

   _____

   _____

Master 8 Life Molecules

Disaccharide (Sucrose)

Polysaccharide (Amylose)

Lipids

Saturated

Unsaturated

Protein

Nucleotide

Phosphate base

Nitrogenous base

5-carbon sugar

Worksheet 8 Life Molecules

1. Explain why carbon atoms are important in organic molecules. Include information about the kinds of bonds carbon can form.

   _____

2. What is the basic definition of a carbohydrate?

   _____

3. What is the difference between a monosaccharide, a disaccharide, and a polysaccharide?

   _____

   _____

4. How do the following carbohydrates function in living things?
   a. starch

   _____

   b. glycogen

   _____

   c. cellulose

   _____

5. What are lipids, and how are they important to living things?

   _____

6. Define the following terms:
   a. protein

   _____

   b. amino acid

   _____

   c. peptide bond

   _____

7. What is the role of proteins in living things?

   _____

   _____

8. Describe the structure of nucleotides and explain how they are important to living things.

   _____

   _____

Chapter 6 — The Chemistry of Life

Reviewing Vocabulary

Match the definition in Column A with the term in Column B.

	Column A	Column B
_____	**1.** Center of an atom	**a.** diffusion
_____	**2.** Mixture in which one or more substances are distributed evenly in another substance	**b.** enzyme
_____	**3.** All of the chemical reactions that occur within an organism	**c.** metabolism
_____	**4.** Bond formed between amino acids	**d.** nucleus
_____	**5.** Protein that changes the rate of a chemical reaction	**e.** peptide bond
_____	**6.** Molecule with unequal distribution of charge	**f.** polar molecule
_____	**7.** Large molecule formed when many smaller molecules bond together	**g.** polymer
_____	**8.** Net movement of particles from an area of higher concentration to an area of lower concentration	**h.** solution

In the space at the left, write the term in parentheses that makes each statement correct.

_____ **9.** Atoms of the same element with different numbers of neutrons are (*isotopes, isomers*).

_____ **10.** Atoms of two or more elements chemically combined are (*mixtures, compounds*).

_____ **11.** Two atoms that share electrons are held together by (*ionic, covalent*) bonds.

_____ **12.** Any substance that forms hydrogen ions in water is a(n) (*acid, base*).

_____ **13.** The smaller subunits that make up nucleic acids are (*amino acids, nucleotides*).

_____ **14.** Some substances move into cells by (*hydrogen bonding, diffusion*).

Chapter
6 **The Chemistry of Life,** *continued*

Chapter Assessment

Understanding Main Ideas (Part A)

In the space at the left, write the letter of the word or phrase that best completes the statement.

_____ **1.** Unlike carbohydrates and lipids, proteins contain

     a. nitrogen.   **b.** carbon.   **c.** hydrogen.   **d.** oxygen.

_____ **2.** A(n) _____ is formed when two atoms share electrons, such as with hydrogen and oxygen in water.

     a. solution   **b.** covalent bond
     c. ionic bond   **d.** isotope

_____ **3.** An atom of fluorine has 9 electrons. Its second energy level has

     a. 2 electrons.   **b.** 8 electrons.   **c.** 7 electrons.   **d.** 9 electrons.

_____ **4.** The total number of atoms in a molecule of sucrose, $C_{12}H_{22}O_{11}$, is

     a. 11.   **b.** 12.   **c.** 22.   **d.** 45.

_____ **5.** Carbon-12, carbon-13, and carbon-14 are

     a. isotopes.   **b.** polymers.   **c.** radioisotopes.   **d.** macromolecules.

_____ **6.** A very strong base might have a pH of

     a. 3.   **b.** 5.   **c.** 9.   **d.** 13.

_____ **7.** Glucose and fructose, both with the formula $C_6H_{12}O_6$, differ in

     a. numbers of atoms.   **b.** arrangement of atoms.
     c. kinds of atoms.   **d.** arrangement of electrons.

_____ **8.** The various enzymes in our bodies are

     a. lipids.   **b.** carbohydrates.   **c.** nucleotides.   **d.** proteins.

_____ **9.** A chlorine atom becomes a chloride ion when it

     a. gains an electron.   **b.** loses an electron.
     c. gains a neutron.   **d.** loses a proton.

_____ **10.** When molecules of glucose and fructose combine to form sucrose, they do so by

     a. hydrolysis.   **b.** electron levels.   **c.** condensation.   **d.** radiation.

_____ **11.** Water dissolves many ionic and molecular compounds because of its

     a. ionic bonding.   **b.** polarity.
     c. capillary action.   **d.** size.

_____ **12.** When there is no difference in the concentration of a substance from one area to another,

     a. diffusion occurs.   **b.** dynamic equilibrium has been reached.
     c. the atoms stop moving.   **d.** there is a concentration gradient.

Chapter
6   **The Chemistry of Life,** *continued*

Understanding Main Ideas (Part B)

Study the diagram, which shows the formation of magnesium chloride and hydrogen fluoride.
Then answer the questions.

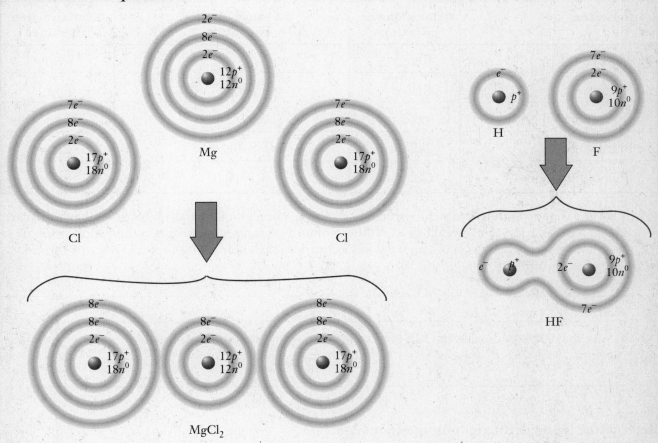

1. Which compound is formed by ionic bonding? Explain.

_____

_____

_____

2. Which compound is formed by covalent bonding? Explain.

_____

_____

3. How many electrons are in the third energy level of a magnesium atom? _____

4. Which atom forms an ion by the loss of electrons? _____

Chapter 6 **The Chemistry of Life,** continued

Chapter Assessment

Thinking Critically

To answer questions 1 and 2, use the table of acid–base indicators below.

Indicator	Color at lower pH values	pH range of color transition	Color at higher pH values
Methyl red	Red	4.4–6.0	Yellow
Litmus	Red	5.5–8.0	Blue
Bromothymol blue	Yellow	6.0–7.6	Blue
Phenol red	Yellow	6.8–8.4	Red
Phenolphthalein	Colorless	8.3–10.0	Red

1. A small volume of dilute hydrochloric acid is placed in a beaker and two drops of phenolphthalein are added. The solution remains colorless. A dilute solution of sodium hydroxide is then added drop by drop until a color change occurs. In what pH range does the color change occur? Describe the color change that occurs.

_____

_____

2. If you exhale carbon dioxide (CO_2) into a solution of bromothymol blue, the solution turns from blue to yellow. Does CO_2 dissolve in water to form an acid or a base?

_____

Refer to the figure at the right for questions 3–5.

3. What type of biological compounds are A and B?

_____

4. Classify A and B as either saturated or unsaturated. Explain.

_____

_____

_____

5. In most lipids, compounds like A and B are attached

to a 3-carbon molecule of _____ .

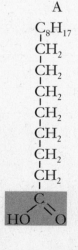

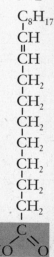

Applying Scientific Methods

Two students carry out an investigation to determine the action of the enzyme pepsin on protein digestion in the human stomach. They know that gastric juice in the stomach contains water, pepsin, and hydrochloric acid. They decide to use small, equal-sized pieces of cooked egg white as the protein to be digested.

They set up four test tubes and place equal small amounts of egg white in each test tube. Then they fill each test tube with a different liquid to a height of 3 centimeters. To test tube 1, they add water; to test tube 2, they add hydrochloric acid (HCl diluted in water); to test tube 3, they add pepsin dissolved in water; and to test tube 4, they add pepsin solution and dilute hydrochloric acid. They place the four test tubes in an incubator set at 37°C (body temperature).

After one day, they observe the results. Then they return the test tubes to the incubator and observe them again the next day. The following table is the record of the results.

Test tube	1 day	2 days
1. egg + water	no change	no change
2. egg + hydrochloric acid	no change	no change
3. egg + pepsin solution	liquid slightly cloudy, egg pieces unchanged	liquid cloudy, egg pieces smaller
4. egg + pepsin solution + hydrochloric acid	liquid cloudy, egg pieces smaller	liquid very cloudy, almost no egg remains

1. Which test tube is the control? Explain its purpose.

_____

_____

_____

2. What is the independent variable in the experiment? The dependent variable?

_____

_____

_____

**Chapter
6** **The Chemistry of Life,** *continued*

Applying Scientific Methods   *continued*

3. What is the hypothesis on which this experiment is based?

_____

_____

_____

4. Was the hypothesis correct? Explain?

_____

_____

_____

5. What kind of results would have shown that the hypothesis is not correct?

_____

_____

_____

_____

6. What did the results from test tube 2 tell about protein digestion in the stomach?

_____

_____

_____

_____

7. Write a conclusion to the experiment. Base your conclusion on the experimental results.

_____

_____

_____

_____

_____

Chapter 6 Assessment
Student Recording Sheet

Use with pages 168–169 of the Student Edition

Vocabulary Review

Write the vocabulary words that match the definitions in your book.

1. _____   3. _____

2. _____   4. _____

Understanding Key Concepts

Select the best answer from the choices given and fill in the corresponding oval.

5. Ⓐ Ⓑ Ⓒ Ⓓ   10. Ⓐ Ⓑ Ⓒ Ⓓ

6. Ⓐ Ⓑ Ⓒ Ⓓ   11. Ⓐ Ⓑ Ⓒ Ⓓ

7. Ⓐ Ⓑ Ⓒ Ⓓ   12. Ⓐ Ⓑ Ⓒ Ⓓ

8. Ⓐ Ⓑ Ⓒ Ⓓ   13. Ⓐ Ⓑ Ⓒ Ⓓ

9. Ⓐ Ⓑ Ⓒ Ⓓ

Constructed Response

Record your answers for Questions 14–16 on a separate sheet of paper.

Thinking Critically

Record your answer for Question 17 on a separate sheet of paper.

18. **REAL WORLD BIOCHALLENGE** Follow your teacher's instructions for presenting your BioChallenge answer.

Standardized Test Practice

The Princeton Review

Part 1   Multiple Choice

Select the best answer from the choices given and fill in the corresponding oval.

19. Ⓐ Ⓑ Ⓒ Ⓓ

20. Ⓐ Ⓑ Ⓒ Ⓓ

21. Ⓐ Ⓑ Ⓒ Ⓓ

22. Ⓐ Ⓑ Ⓒ Ⓓ

23. Ⓐ Ⓑ Ⓒ Ⓓ

Part 2
Constructed Response/Grid In

Record your answers for Questions 24 and 25 on a separate sheet of paper.

Chapter 7 A View of the Cell

Chapter 7

MiniLab 7.1 — Measuring Objects Under a Microscope

Measuring in SI

Knowing the diameter of the circle of light you see when looking through a microscope allows you to measure the size of objects that are being viewed. For most microscopes, the diameter of the circle of light is 1.5 mm, or 1500 μm (micrometers), under low power and 0.375 mm, or 375 μm, under high power.

Refer to *Practicing Scientific Methods* in the **Skill Handbook** if you need help with SI units.

Procedure

1 Look at diagram A on page 173 of your text that shows an object viewed under low power. Knowing the circle diameter to be 1500 μm, the estimated length of object (a) is 400 μm. What is the estimated length of object (b)?

_____

2 Look at diagram B on page 173 of your text that shows an object viewed under high power. Knowing the circle diameter to be 375 μm, the estimated length of object (c) is 100 μm. What is the estimated length of object (d)?

_____

3 Prepare a wet mount of a strand of your hair. Your teacher can help with this procedure. **CAUTION:** *Use caution when handling microscopes and glass slides.* Measure the width of your hair strand while viewing it under low and then high power.

_____

Analysis

1. An object can be magnified 100, 200, or 1000 times when viewed under a microscope. Does the object's actual size change with each magnification? Explain.

_____

_____

_____

2. Do your observations of the diameter of your hair strand under low and high power support the answer to question 1? If not, offer a possible explanation why.

_____

_____

_____

MiniLab 7.2   Cell Organelles

Experimenting

Adding stains to cellular material helps you distinguish cell organelles.

Procedure

CAUTION: *Be sure to wash hands before and after this experiment.*

1 Prepare a water wet mount of onion skin. Do this by using your fingernail to peel off the inside of a layer of onion bulb. The layer must be almost transparent. Use the diagram on page 182 of your text as a guide.

2 Make sure that the onion layer is laying flat on the glass slide and is not folded.

3 Observe the onion cells under low- and high-power magnification. Identify as many organelles as possible.

4 Repeat steps 1 through 3, only this time use an iodine stain instead of water.

Analysis

1. What organelles were easily seen in the unstained onion cells? In cells stained with iodine?

_____

_____

2. How are stains useful for viewing cells?

_____

_____

Observing and Comparing Different Cell Types

Chapter 7

Problem
Are all cells alike in appearance and size?

Objectives
In this BioLab, you will:
- **Observe**, **diagram**, and **measure** cells and their organelles.
- **Infer** which cells are prokaryotic or eukaryotic and whether they are from unicellular organisms and multicellular organisms.
- **List** the traits of plant and animal cells.

Materials
microscope	dropper
glass slide	coverslip
water	forceps

prepared slides of *Bacillus subtilis*, frog blood, and *Elodea*

Safety Precautions
Always wear goggles in the lab.

Skill Handbook
Use the **Skill Handbook** if you need additional help with this lab.

1. Use the data table below.
2. Examine a prepared slide of *Bacillus subtilis* using both low- and high-power magnification. (NOTE: This slide has been stained.

Bacterial cells have no natural color.)
CAUTION: *Use care when handling slides. Dispose of any broken glass in a container provided by your teacher.*

Data Table

	Bacillus subtilis	*Elodea*	Frog Blood
Organelles observed			
Prokaryote or eukaryote			
From a multicellular or unicellular organism			
Diagram (with size in micrometers, μm)			

Observing and Comparing Different Cell Types, *continued*

3. Look for and record the names of any observed organelles. Infer whether these cells are prokaryotes or eukaryotes. Infer whether these cells are from a unicellular or multicellular organism. Record your findings in the table.
4. Diagram one cell as seen under high-power magnification.
5. While using high power, determine the length and width in micrometers of this cell. Refer to *Thinking Critically* in the **Skill Handbook** for help with determining magnification. Record your measurements on the diagram.
6. Prepare a wet mount of a single leaf from *Elodea* using the diagram as a guide.

7. Observe cells under low- and high-power magnification.
8. Repeat steps 3 through 5 for *Elodea*.
9. Examine a prepared slide of frog blood. (NOTE: This slide has been stained. Its natural color is pink.)
10. Observe cells under low- and high-power magnification.
11. Repeat steps 3 through 5 for frog blood cells.
12. **Cleanup and Disposal** Clean all equipment as instructed by your teacher, and return everything to its proper place for reuse. Wash your hands thoroughly.

ANALYZE AND CONCLUDE

1. **Observing and Inferring** Which cells were prokaryotic and which were eukaryotic? How were you able to tell?

_____

_____

2. **Predicting** Which cell was from a plant, from an animal? Explain your answer.

_____

_____

3. **Measuring** Are prokaryotic or eukaryotic cells larger? Give specific measurements to support your answer.

_____

_____

_____

4. **Defining Operationally** Compare the structure and function of the plant and animal cells you saw.

_____

_____

_____

5. **Error Analysis** Suppose you estimate that eight *Elodea* cells will fit across the high-power field of view of your microscope. You calculate that the diameter of an *Elodea* cell is approximately 50 mm. Is this a reasonable value? If not, what was the error in your analysis?

_____

_____

Chapter 7 — Inside the Artificial Kidney Machine

Real World BioApplications

One of the most important organs in vertebrates is the kidney. Kidneys, which occur in pairs, help maintain homeostasis by regulating the concentrations of dissolved substances in the blood. Without this constant monitoring by the kidneys, the nitrogenous waste products of cellular activity can build to toxic concentrations. It is possible to live with only one kidney; however, if both kidneys fail, people must have their blood filtered by an artificial kidney machine in a process called hemodialysis. In this activity, you will investigate how artificial kidney machines duplicate the important functions of kidneys.

Part A: Nephron Structure and Function

Each kidney is composed of nearly one million tiny filtering units called nephrons (Figure 1). Through a complex process involving both active and passive transport of substances, nephrons filter out excess water, waste molecules, and excess ions from the blood, and ensure that critical nutrients such as glucose and proteins remain in the blood. The table in Figure 1 shows how the concentrations of substances dissolved in the blood change as they pass through the kidney. Study the table and diagram of the nephron in Figure 1, and then answer the following questions.

Concentrations of Dissolved Substances (mg/100 mL of fluid)			
Dissolved Substances	Arterial Blood (A)	Filtrate (B)	Urine (C)
Urea	30	30	2000
Uric Acid	2	2	30
Glucose	100	100	0
Salts	900	900	2300
Protein	8500	0	0

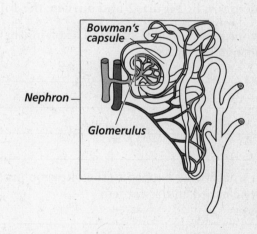

Figure 1

1. Bowman's capsule is a selectively permeable structure. According to the table, which substances pass through Bowman's capsule into the tubule to become filtrate?

_____

2. Which parts of the nephron actually filter the blood?

_____

3. Using your understanding of diffusion, how might you account for the increases in concentration of urea, uric acid, and salts in urine?

_____

_____

4. What happened to the glucose in the filtrate? What process was involved?

_____

Chapter 7 | **Inside the Artificial Kidney Machine**

Real World BioApplications

Part B: How Do Artificial Kidney Machines Work?

Artificial kidney machines, like kidneys, work by the process of diffusion. During dialysis, blood is pumped from a person's artery through selectively permeable tubing that is bathed in a solution similar to actual blood plasma. As the blood circulates through the tubing, waste materials diffuse from the tubing into the surrounding solution and are washed away. The cleaned blood left behind is then returned to a vein.

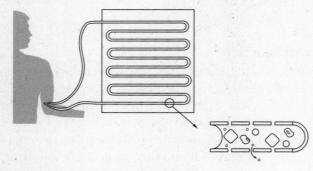

Figure 2

Study the diagram in Figure 2 and answer the following questions.

1. Using your knowledge of diffusion, explain what happens to the waste materials as the blood circulates through the machine.

   _____

   _____

   _____

   _____

2. Explain what would happen to the diffusion process if the solution surrounding the tubing were not regularly cleaned and discarded.

   _____

   _____

   _____

3. Which molecules would you expect to find in the tube leading back from the machine to the person's vein?

   _____

   _____

4. Explain why blood cells, glucose, protein, salts, and water don't leave the tubing.

   _____

   _____

   _____

   _____

Name _____ Date _____ Class _____

In your textbook, read about the history of the cell theory.

For each statement in Column A, write the letter of the matching item in Column B.

	Column A	Column B
_____	**1.** The first scientist to describe living cells as seen through a simple microscope	**a.** Schleiden
_____	**2.** Uses two or more glass lenses to magnify either living cells or prepared slides	**b.** compound light microscope
_____	**3.** A scientist who observed that cork was composed of tiny, hollow boxes that he called cells	**c.** electron microscope
_____	**4.** A scientist who concluded that all plants are composed of cells	**d.** Schwann
_____	**5.** A scientist who concluded that all animals are composed of cells	**e.** Hooke
_____	**6.** The microscope that allowed scientists to view molecules	**f.** van Leeuwenhoek

In your textbook, read about the two basic cell types.

Complete the table by checking the correct column for each statement.

Statement	Prokaryotes	Eukaryotes
7. Organisms that have cells lacking internal membrane-bound structures		
8. Do not have a nucleus		
9. Are either single-celled or made up of many cells		
10. Generally are single-celled organisms		
11. Organisms that have cells containing organelles		

In your textbook, read about maintaining a balance.

Use each of the terms below just once to complete the passage.

glucose	plasma membrane	homeostasis
organism	balance	selective permeability

Living cells maintain a **(1)** _____ by controlling materials that enter and leave. Without this

ability, the cell cannot maintain **(2)** _____ and will die. The cell must regulate internal con-

centrations of water, **(3)** _____ , and other nutrients and must eliminate waste products.

Homeostasis in a cell is maintained by the **(4)** _____ , which allows only certain

particles to pass through and keeps other particles out. This property of a membrane is known as

(5) _____ . It allows different cells to carry on different activities within the

same **(6)** _____ .

In your textbook, read about the structure of the plasma membrane.

For each statement below, write <u>true</u> or <u>false</u>.

_____ **7.** The structure and properties of the cell wall allow it to be selective and maintain homeostasis.

_____ **8.** The plasma membrane is a bilayer of lipid molecules with protein molecules embedded in it.

_____ **9.** A phospholipid molecule has a nonpolar, water-insoluble head attached to a long polar, soluble tail.

_____ **10.** The fluid mosaic model describes the plasma membrane as a structure that is liquid and very rigid.

_____ **11.** Eukaryotic plasma membranes can contain cholesterol, which tends to make the membrane more stable.

_____ **12.** Transport proteins span the cell membrane, allowing the selectively perme-able membrane to regulate which molecules enter and leave a cell.

_____ **13.** Proteins at the inner surface of the plasma membrane attach the membrane to the cell's support structure, making the cell rigid.

Reinforcement and Study Guide

Section 7.3 Eukaryotic Cell Structure

In your textbook, read about cellular boundaries; nucleus and cell control; assembly, transport, and storage in the cell; and energy transformers.

Complete the table by writing the name of the cell part beside its structure/function. A cell part may be used more than once.

Structure/Function	Cell Part
1. A membrane-bound, fluid-filled sac	
2. Closely stacked, flattened membrane sacs	
3. The sites of protein synthesis	
4. A folded membrane that forms a network of interconnected compartments in the cytoplasm	
5. The clear fluid inside the cell	
6. Organelle that manages cell functions in eukaryotic cell	
7. Contains chlorophyll, a green pigment that traps energy from sunlight and gives plants their green color	
8. Digest excess or worn-out cell parts, food particles, and invading viruses or bacteria	
9. Small bumps located on the endoplasmic reticulum	
10. Provides temporary storage of food, enzymes, and waste products	
11. Firm, protective structure that gives the cell its shape in plants, fungi, most bacteria, and some protists	
12. Produce a usable form of energy for the cell	
13. Modifies proteins chemically, then repackages them	
14. Contains inner membranes arranged in stacks of membranous sacs called grana	
15. Plant organelles that store starches or lipids or that contain pigments	

Chapter 7 **A View of the Cell,** *continued*

In your textbook, read about structures for support and locomotion.

Determine if the statement is true. If it is not, rewrite the italicized part to make it true.

16. Cells have a support structure within the *cytoplasm* called the cytoskeleton.

_____

17. The *exoskeleton* is composed of thin, fibrous elements that form a framework for the cell.

_____

18. *Microtubules* of the cytoskeleton are thin, hollow cylinders made of protein.

_____

19. Cilia and flagella are cell surface structures that are adapted for *respiration*.

_____

20. *Flagella* are short, numerous, hairlike projections from the plasma membrane.

_____

21. Flagella are longer and *more* numerous than cilia.

_____

22. In *multicellular* organisms, cilia and flagella are the major means of locomotion.

_____

23. In *prokaryotic* cells, both cilia and flagella are composed of microtubules.

_____

Write titles for each of the generalized diagrams and then label the parts. Use these choices: plant cell, animal cell, plasma membrane, chloroplast, lysosome, large vacuole, cell wall.

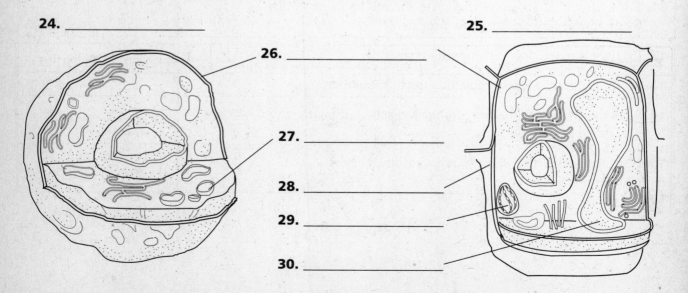

24. _____

25. _____

26. _____

27. _____

28. _____

29. _____

30. _____

Capítulo 7
Un vistazo a la célula
Sección 7.1 El descubrimiento de la célula

En tu libro de texto, lee sobre la historia de la teoría celular.

Anota la letra de la columna B que corresponde a cada enunciado de la columna A.

Columna A	Columna B
_____ **1.** El primer científico que describió las células, vistas a través de un microscopio simple	**a.** Schleiden
_____ **2.** Usa dos lentes para aumentar el tamaño de las imágenes de células vivas o de laminillas preparadas	**b.** microscopio óptico compuesto
_____ **3.** Científico que observó que el corcho estaba formado por celdillas vacías que denominó células	**c.** microscopio electrónico
_____ **4.** Científico que concluyó que todas las plantas estaban formadas por células	**d.** Schwann
_____ **5.** Científico que concluyó que todos los animales estaban formados por células	**e.** Hooke
_____ **6.** Microscopio que permitió a los científicos observar moléculas	**f.** van Leeuwenhoek

En tu libro de texto, lee sobre los dos tipos básicos de células.

Completa la tabla indicando la columna correspondiente a cada enunciado.

Enunciado	Procariotas	Eucariotas
7. Organismos formados por células que carecen de estructuras membranosas internas		
8. No tienen núcleo		
9. Están formados por una o muchas células		
10. En general son organismos unicelulares		
11. Organismos formados por células que tienen organelos		

Capítulo 7 Un vistazo a la célula, *continuación*

En tu libro de texto, lee sobre cómo mantiene la célula el equilibrio.

Usa cada término una sola vez para completar el párrafo.

glucosa   membrana plasmática   homeostasis

organismo   equilibrio   permeabilidad selectiva

Las células vivas mantienen un **(1)** _____ controlando los materiales que entran y salen de ella. Si

carecieran de esta capacidad, las células no podrían mantener su **(2)** _____ y morirían. La

célula debe regular la concentración interna de agua, **(3)** _____ y otros nutrientes y debe

también eliminar sus desechos. La **(4)** _____ mantiene la homeostasis de la célula, lo

cual permite que sólo ciertas partículas entren a la célula y evita que otras salgan. Esta propiedad de la

célula se conoce como **(5)** _____ y ayuda a que diferentes células cumplan

diferentes funciones dentro de un mismo **(6)** _____ .

En tu libro de texto, lee sobre la estructura de la membrana plasmática.

Indica si cada enunciado es <u>verdadero</u> o <u>falso</u>.

_____ **7.** La estructura y las propiedades de la pared celular le permiten ser selectiva y mantener la homeostasis.

_____ **8.** La membrana plasmática es una capa doble de moléculas de lípidos con proteínas incrustadas.

_____ **9.** La molécula de un fosfolípido tiene una cabeza no polar, insoluble en agua, unida al extremo o cola que es polar y soluble.

_____ **10.** El modelo del mosaico fluido describe la membrana plasmática como una estructura líquida y muy rígida.

_____ **11.** La membrana plasmática de las células eucariotas puede contener colesterol, lo que ayuda a una mayor estabilidad en las membranas.

_____ **12.** Las proteínas de transporte atraviesan la membrana celular y le confieren permeabilidad selectiva que regula las moléculas que entran y salen de la célula.

_____ **13.** Las proteínas de la superficie interna de la membrana plasmática unen la membrana a la estructura de soporte de la célula, haciendo que la célula sea rígida.

Nombre   Fecha   Clase

Capítulo 7   Un vistazo a la célula, *continuación*

Refuerzo y Guía de estudio

Sección 7.3 Estructura de la célula eucariótica

En tu libro de texto, lee sobre los límites de la célula; el núcleo y el control celular; el ensamblaje, el transporte y el almacenamiento en la célula y los transformadores de energía.

Completa la tabla escribiendo el nombre de la parte de la célula que corresponde a cada descripción en la primera columna. Se puede usar cada parte más de una vez.

Estructura/Función	Parte de la célula
1. Saco membranoso lleno de fluido	
2. Sacos membranosos planos y semejantes a monedas apiladas	
3. Sitio donde ocurre la síntesis de proteínas	
4. Membrana plegada que forma dentro del citoplasma una red de compartimientos interconectados	
5. Fluido claro dentro de la célula	
6. Organelo que controla las funciones de las células eucariotas	
7. Contiene clorofila, un pigmento verde que atrapa la energía de la luz solar y que proporciona a las plantas su color verde	
8. Digiere las partes gastadas o sobrantes de una célula, las partículas alimenticias y los virus o bacterias	
9. Pequeños gránulos localizados en el retículo endoplásmico	
10. Sirve como almacén temporal de alimentos, enzimas y desechos	
11. Estructura protectora firme que da forma a las células de plantas, hongos, la mayoría de las bacterias y algunos protistas	
12. Produce una forma de energía que la célula puede usar	
13. Modifica químicamente las proteínas y las envuelve o empaca	
14. Contiene membranas internas que forman una estructura con forma de sacos planos apilados llamados grana	
15. Organelos de la planta que almacenan almidones o lípidos, o que contienen pigmentos	

UNIDAD 3   CAPÍTULO 7   Un vistazo a la célula   **53**

Nombre _____   Fecha _____   Clase _____

Capítulo 7 — Un vistazo a la célula, *continuación*

Refuerzo y Guía de estudio

Sección 7.3 Estructura de la célula eucariótica

En tu libro de texto, lee acerca de las estructuras de sostén y locomoción.

Si el enunciado es verdadero, escribe *verdadero*; de lo contrario, modifica la sección en itálicas para hacer verdadero el enunciado.

16. Las células poseen una estructura de soporte dentro del *citoplasma* llamada citoesqueleto.

_____

17. El *exoesqueleto* está compuesto de elementos fibrosos y delgados que dan forma a la célula.

_____

18. Los *microtúbulos* del citoesqueleto son cilindros delgados y huecos compuestos de proteína.

_____

19. Los cilios y los flagelos son estructuras de la superficie de la célula adaptadas para la *respiración celular*.

_____

20. Los *flagelos* son proyecciones cortas y numerosas de la membrana plasmática.

_____

21. Los flagelos son más largos y *más* numerosos que los cilios.

_____

22. En los organismos *multicelulares*, los cilios y los flagelos son los principales medios de locomoción.

_____

23. Los cilios y flagelos de las células *procariotas* están compuestos de microtúbulos.

_____

Identifica el tipo de célula representado por cada diagrama y rotula las partes. Usa estos términos: célula vegetal, célula animal, membrana plasmática, cloroplasto, vacuola pequeña, vacuola grande y pared celular.

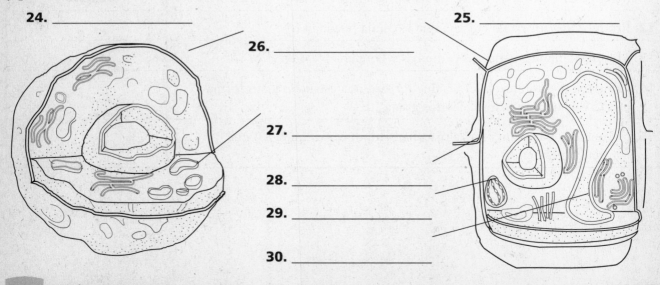

24. _____   25. _____   26. _____   27. _____   28. _____   29. _____   30. _____

54   CAPÍTULO 7   Un vistazo a la célula   UNIDAD 3

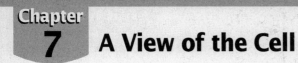

Chapter 7 A View of the Cell

Concept Mapping

Use with Chapter 7, Section 7.3

Recycling in the Cell

Complete the concept map on recycling in a cell. Use these words or phrases one or more times: *lysosomes, food particles, a membrane, bacteria and viruses, cell proteins, tail, vacuoles, worn-out cell parts, digesting it, digestive enzymes.*

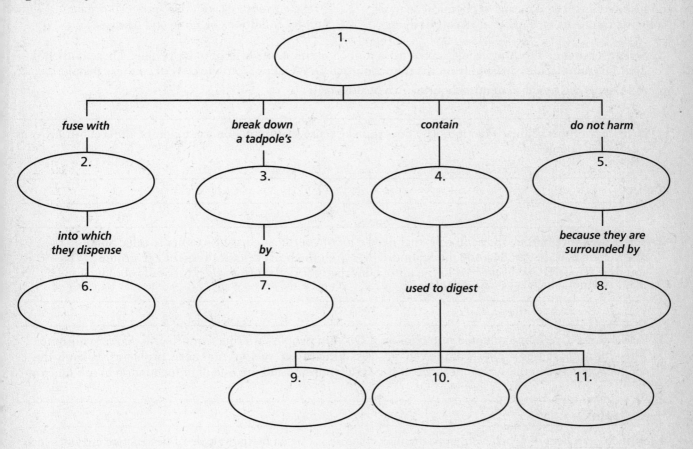

Chapter 7 — A View of the Cell

Critical Thinking

Use with Chapter 7, Section 7.3

Cell Organelles and Their Functions

In the past, biologists looked for clues to aging and human disease by studying organs, tissues, and cultures of cells. With more powerful microscopes and more sophisticated means of chemical analysis, biologists can focus on smaller elements of living things: the organelles within individual cells. Use your knowledge of cell organelles and their functions to answer the following questions about some of the current research that links cell organelles with certain conditions of aging and disease.

1. Scientists studied DNA molecules taken from mitochondria in the cells of older people. These mitochondrial DNA molecules differed from the mitochondrial DNA taken from the cells of younger people.

   a. What is the function of mitochondria in a healthy cell?

   _____

   b. In view of this cellular function, why does it make sense that mitochondria might be different in the cells of older people?

   _____

   _____

   _____

2. There are more mitochondria in cells that need a lot of energy, such as heart muscle cells. Some researchers have begun to study mitochondrial DNA in the heart cells of different age groups. What do you think researchers discovered in the mitochondrial DNA taken from the heart cells of older adults?

   _____

   _____

3. Researchers have found mutated mitochondrial DNA in people suffering from Kearns-Sayre syndrome. The syndrome causes paralysis of the eye muscles, difficulty in walking, and heart problems. What is the connection between the symptoms of Kearns-Sayre syndrome and the role of mitochondria in cell function?

   _____

   _____

4. Some researchers now believe that Alzheimer's disease is caused by the release of destructive enzymes into the cytoplasm of nerve cells. The enzymes are thought to be released by organelles whose membranes ruptured as they were trying to digest harmful proteins. Which organelles do you think are responsible for the release of these destructive enzymes? Why?

   _____

5. In the liver cells of a person who died from alcoholism, an extremely dense network of smooth endoplasmic reticulum was found. Why do you think this was so? Hint: Smooth ER has enzymes that break down harmful substances, or toxins, in the liver.

   _____

   _____

   _____

   _____

Master 15 Section Focus

Gathering Information with Scientific Tools

Use with Chapter 7, Section 7.1

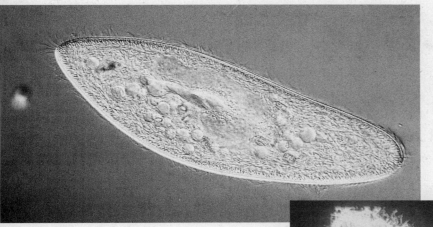

M. Abbey/Visuals Unlimited

A) Stained LM magnification: 110x

B) Color-enhanced SEM magnification: 1500x

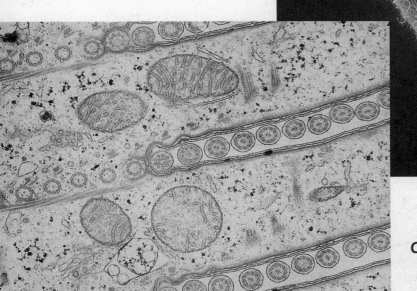

T.E. Adams/Visuals Unlimited

Dr. Kari Lounatmaa/Science Photo Library/Photo Researchers

C) Color-enhanced TEM magnification: 41 500x

❶ The images have been made by three different types of microscopes. How do the images differ?

❷ What kinds of information might scientists gather with each type of microscope?

Master

16   Movement of Materials

Use with Chapter 7, Section 7.2

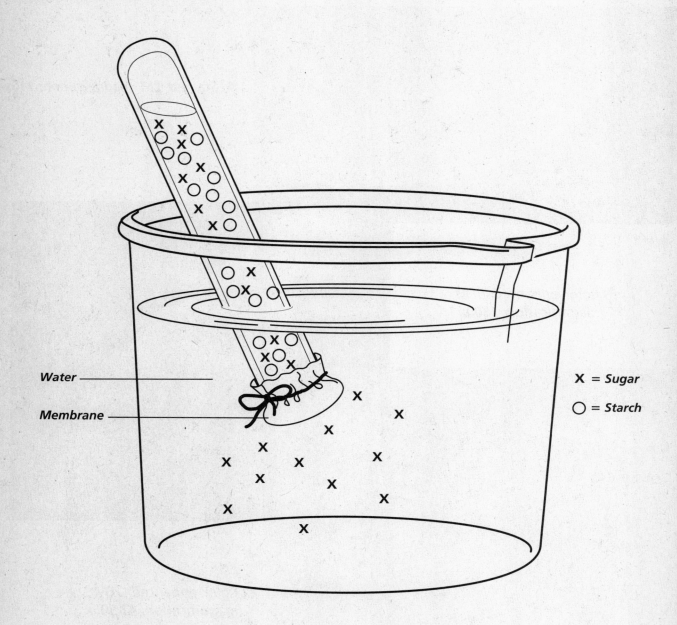

Water

Membrane

X = Sugar

O = Starch

1 What is happening to the starch and the sugar?

2 What does this tell you about the membrane covering the test tube?

Master
17 **Plant and Animal Cells**

Use with Chapter 7, Section 7.3

CORBIS

PhotoDisc/Getty Images

1 What do plants and animals need to stay alive?

2 Name some ways plant and animal cells would be similar.
Name some differences. Why do you think that?

Master 6   Plasma Membrane

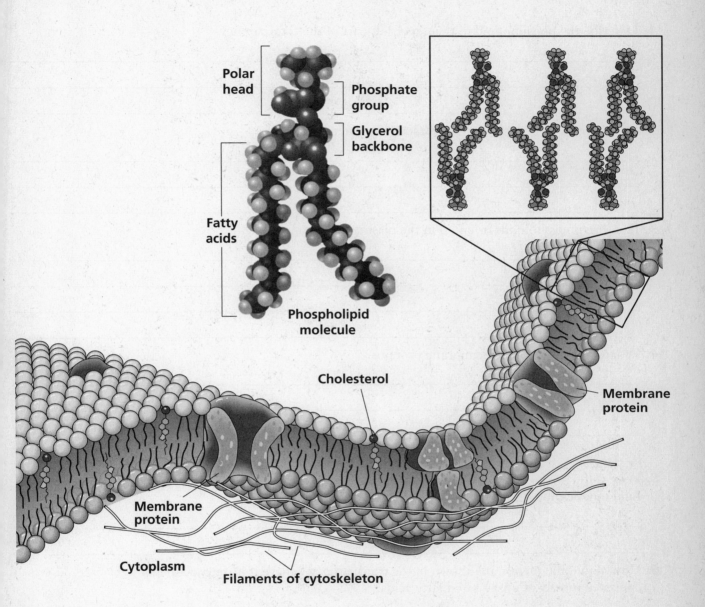

Polar head

Phosphate group

Glycerol backbone

Fatty acids

Phospholipid molecule

Cholesterol

Membrane protein

Membrane protein

Cytoplasm

Filaments of cytoskeleton

Worksheet 6 — Plasma Membrane

1. Describe the phospholipid in the upper left part of the transparency.

_____

_____

_____

2. Which end of a phospholipid is attracted to water?

_____

_____

3. How are phospholipids oriented in the plasma membrane?

_____

_____

_____

_____

4. What is the function of membrane proteins?

_____

_____

_____

5. Why is the model of a membrane shown in the transparency referred to as the fluid mosaic model?

_____

_____

6. How would the membrane shown in the transparency behave if its fatty acid tails consisted mostly of unsaturated fatty acids?

_____

_____

7. What is the function of the cholesterol molecules shown in the transparency?

_____

_____

_____

Master

7   The Cell

Basic Concepts

Use with Chapter 7, Section 7.3

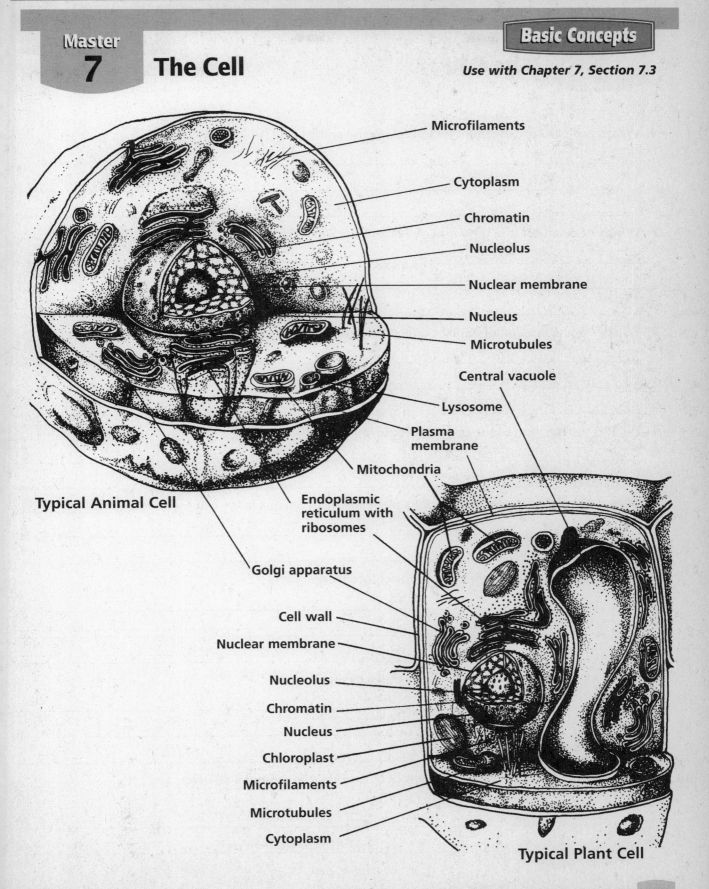

Microfilaments

Cytoplasm

Chromatin

Nucleolus

Nuclear membrane

Nucleus

Microtubules

Central vacuole

Lysosome

Plasma membrane

Mitochondria

Endoplasmic reticulum with ribosomes

Typical Animal Cell

Golgi apparatus

Cell wall

Nuclear membrane

Nucleolus

Chromatin

Nucleus

Chloroplast

Microfilaments

Microtubules

Cytoplasm

Typical Plant Cell

The Cell

1. Which cell parts are common to both plant and animal cells?

_____

_____

_____

2. Which organelle aids in digestion of worn-out cell parts?

_____

_____

_____

3. Which organelle is found in plant cells but not in animal cells?

_____

_____

_____

4. What is the function of the central vacuole in plant cells?

_____

_____

5. What would be the likely function of a plant cell that contains many chloroplasts?

_____

_____

6. Which plant cells might not contain any chloroplasts?

_____

_____

_____

7. Which organelles are produced within the nucleolus?

_____

_____

_____

8. Why would a cell that moves by means of cilia or flagella require a relatively large number of mitochondria?

_____

_____

Master
9

The Optical Microscope

Use with Chapter 7, Section 7.1

Eyepieces
Contain magnifying lenses
to look through

Arm

Low-power objective
Contains the lens with
low power magnification

Revolving nosepiece
Holds and turns the
objectives into viewing
position

Stage clips
Holds the microscope
slide in place

High-power objectives
Contain lenses with
greater powers of
magnification

Coarse adjustment
Focuses the image
under low power

Stage
Supports the microscope
slide

Fine adjustment
Sharpens the image under
high and low magnification

Diaphragm
Regulates the amount of
light that passes through
the specimen

Light source
Allows light to reflect
upward through the
diaphragm, the specimen,
and the lenses

Worksheet 9 — The Optical Microscope

Reteaching Skills

Use with Chapter 7, Section 7.1

1. What is the function of the diaphragm?

2. If you want to change the objective lens through which you are viewing a specimen, what must you do?

3. What knob is turned to focus an image under low power?

4. What is the purpose of having a light source on a microscope?

5. Explain the significance of the term *compound* in describing a modern light microscope.

6. Identify the parts of the microscope that are used for supporting the specimen and holding it in place.

7. If the magnifying power of an eyepiece is 10× and that of an objective is 45×, by how much is a specimen magnified through this combination of lenses?

8. What is the fundamental difference between a compound microscope and the simple microscope that van Leeuwenhoek used in the 1600s to describe living cells?

9. What major advantage does a transmission electron microscope have over a compound light microscope? What is its major disadvantage?

Master 10

Eukaryotic Cell Structure and Organelles

Use with Chapter 7, Section 7.3

Animal Cell

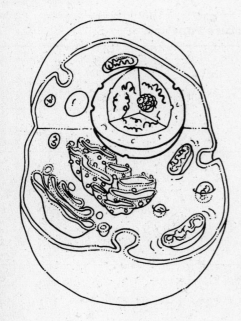

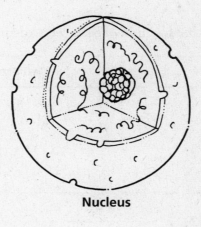

Nucleus

Mitochondrion

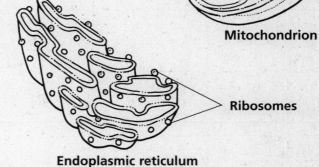

Ribosomes

Endoplasmic reticulum

Golgi apparatus

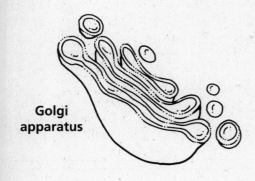

Plasma membrane

Microtubule

Microfilaments

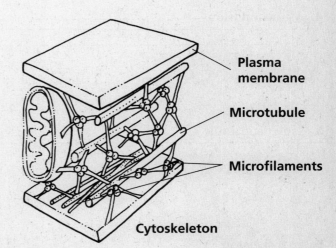

Cytoskeleton

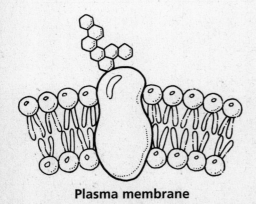

Plasma membrane

Worksheet 10
Eukaryotic Cell Structure and Organelles

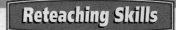
Reteaching Skills

Use with Chapter 7, Section 7.3

In the space provided, describe the function of each cell structure:

Cell Structure	Cell Structure Function
1. Nucleus	
2. Plasma membrane	
3. Endoplasmic reticulum	
4. Mitochondrion	
5. Golgi apparatus	
6. Cytoskeleton	

Chapter 7 — A View of the Cell

Reviewing Vocabulary

Write the word or phrase that best completes the statement.

1. A structure outside the plasma membrane in some cells is the _____ .

2. The functions of a eukaryotic cell are managed by the _____ .

3. In a cell, the tangles of long strands of DNA form the _____ .

4. The folded system of membranes that forms a network of interconnected compartments inside the cell is called the _____ .

5. The pigment that gives plants their green color is _____ .

6. The network of tiny rods and filaments that forms a framework for the cell is called the

   _____ .

7. In plants, the structures that transform light energy into chemical energy are called

   _____ .

In the space at the left, write the term in parentheses that makes each statement correct.

_____ 8. (*Phospholipids, Transport proteins*) make up the selectively permeable membrane that controls which molecules enter and leave the cell.

_____ 9. Short projections used for oarlike locomotion are (*cilia, flagella*).

_____ 10. In a cell, the breakdown of molecules in order to release energy occurs in the (*mitochondria, Golgi apparatus*).

_____ 11. An organism with a cell that lacks a true nucleus is a(n) (*prokaryote, eukaryote*).

_____ 12. The movement of materials into and out of the cells is controlled by the (*cytoplasm, plasma membrane*).

_____ 13. The small, membrane-bound structures inside a cell are (*chromatin, organelles*).

_____ 14. In a cell, the sites of protein synthesis are the (*ribosomes, nucleolus*).

_____ 15. Cell structures that contain digestive enzymes are (*plastids, lysosomes*).

Understanding Concepts (Part A)

In the space at the left, write the letter of the word or phrase that best completes the statement.

_____ **1.** Cell walls of multicellular plants are composed mainly of

         a. cellulose.   **b.** chitin.   **c.** pectin.   **d.** vacuoles.

_____ **2.** The term *least* closely related to the others is

         a. cytoskeleton.   **b.** microfilament.

         c. microtubule.   **d.** cell juncture.

_____ **3.** In a chloroplast, the stacks of membranous sacs are called

         a. stroma.   **b.** grana.

         c. plastids.   **d.** thylakoid membrane.

_____ **4.** The structure most responsible for maintaining cell homeostasis is the

         a. cytoplasm.   **b.** mitochondrion.   **c.** cell wall.   **d.** plasma membrane.

_____ **5.** If a cell contains a nucleus, it must be a(n)

         a. plant cell.   **b.** eukaryotic cell.

         c. animal cell.   **d.** prokaryotic cell.

_____ **6.** One advantage of electron microscopes over light microscopes is their

         a. size.   **b.** higher magnification.

         c. two-dimensional image.   **d.** use of live specimens.

_____ **7.** When a cell is ready to reproduce, its DNA is packed into

         a. chromosomes.   **b.** chromatin.   **c.** nucleoli.   **d.** nucleoids.

_____ **8.** The scientist who first described living cells as seen through a simple microscope was

         a. van Leeuwenhoek.   **b.** Schleiden.

         c. Hooke.   **d.** Schwann.

_____ **9.** Each of the following is a main idea of the cell theory *except*

         a. all organisms are composed of cells.

         b. the cell is the basic unit of organization of organisms.

         c. all cells are similar in structure and function.

         d. all cells come from preexisting cells.

_____ **10.** A plasma membrane is made up of a(n)

         a. cholesterol layer.   **b.** enzyme bilayer.

         c. phospholipid bilayer.   **d.** protein layer.

Chapter 7 **A View of the Cell,** *continued*

Understanding Concepts (Part B)

The diagram below of a bacterium shows a light area with no surrounding membrane in the center of the cell. This area contains a single large DNA molecule. Use the diagram to answer questions 1 and 2.

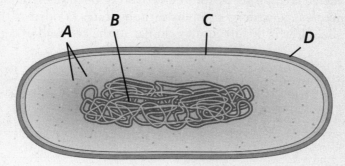

1. Identify the structures labeled A, B, C, and D.

_____

2. Based on the diagram, would scientists classify this cell as a prokaryote or a eukaryote? Explain.

_____
_____
_____
_____

Answer the following questions.

3. In plants, cells that transport water against the force of gravity are found to contain many more mitochondria than do some other plant cells. What is the reason for this?

_____
_____
_____
_____
_____

4. Why did it take almost 200 years after Hooke discovered cells for the cell theory to be developed?

_____
_____
_____
_____

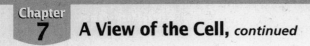

Chapter Assessment

Thinking Critically

Answer the following questions.

1. Many types of animal cells have a thin, flexible cell covering outside the plasma membrane. This cell covering, called a glycocalyx, consists of complex carbohydrates bonded to the proteins and lipids in the plasma membrane. How is the glycocalyx similar to the cell wall of a green plant? How is it different?

_____

_____

_____

_____

_____

2. The stomach lining contains mucus, which helps prevent the digestion of the stomach lining. If this mechanism fails, digestive enzymes in the stomach cause the stomach to digest itself, producing an ulcer. Compare this process with the way lysosomes prevent destruction of the cell's proteins.

_____

_____

_____

_____

_____

3. Between which cell types is the difference greater—plant and animal cells or prokaryotic and eukaryotic cells? Give reasons for your answer.

_____

_____

_____

_____

_____

_____

_____

_____

Applying Scientific Methods

For many years, scientists thought of the nucleus as "a bag of chromatin floating in a sea of cytoplasm." Using electron microscopes, scientists saw that the nucleus was much more complex. The nuclear envelope was two-layered and covered with pores.

Scientists began further research. Scientist S punched small holes in the nuclear envelope, allowing the contents to pour out. He observed that the nucleus retained its spherical shape. From this, scientist S hypothesized that the nucleus had some other structural framework, beyond the membrane itself. The next experiment performed by scientist S revealed that the nucleus indeed had a fibrous protein framework, now called the nuclear matrix.

Three other scientists repeated this experiment, but each changed one part of it. Scientist X used detergents and salt to remove the nuclear contents. Scientist Y used chemicals, and scientist Z used enzymes. All three observed that a nuclear matrix remained.

Further electron microscopy revealed that the chromatin strands are anchored to a fibrous layer that lines the inner layer of the nuclear envelope.

1. What was the hypothesis of scientist S in his first experiment?

_____

2. What observation from scientist S's second experiment supported the original hypothesis?

_____

_____

3. Why did scientists X, Y, and Z carry out their experiments?

_____

_____

4. What was the variable in the experiments by scientists X, Y, and Z?

_____

_____

_____

5. Why did scientists X, Y, and Z use different substances to remove the nuclear contents?

_____

_____

_____

6. Describe a procedure to determine whether the attachment of the chromatin to the nuclear envelope is necessary for the chromatin to become chromosomes.

_____

_____

_____

Chapter
7 **A View of the Cell,** *continued*

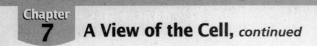

Applying Scientific Methods

In the 1890s, E. Overton performed experiments to determine the structure of the plasma membrane. After many years and various procedures, he determined that large, uncharged molecules enter a cell at a rate proportional to their solubility in lipids. This observation was the first indication that the plasma membrane is probably made up of lipids. Many scientists began to pursue the question of how the lipids were arranged.

In 1925, two Dutch scientists determined that the area covered by the lipids from a single red blood cell is twice the area of the surface of the cell. From this, they reasoned that the cell is covered by a double layer of lipid molecules. Based on this work, various scientists hypothesized that the membrane was like a "fat sandwich" with two outer layers of protein on the surface of the lipid layer.

None of the ideas seemed a satisfactory explanation until microscopic studies of membranes prepared by a new technique of "freeze-fracture" revealed that the proteins are actually embedded in the lipid layer. In 1972, on the basis of these results and other evidence, two American scientists proposed the fluid-mosaic model.

7. What was the problem that Overton was trying to solve with his experiments?

_____

8. Is his hypothesis stated in the discussion above? If so, what was it?

_____

9. The result of one experiment often leads to further experiments. How do Overton's experiments illustrate this fact?

_____

_____

10. What conclusion did the Dutch scientists reach?

_____

11. What inference did the Dutch scientists make to reach their conclusion?

_____

_____

12. What model of the plasma membrane was based on their results?

_____

13. Why was it almost 50 years between the Dutch scientists' research and the proposal of a fluid mosaic model?

_____

_____

_____

Chapter Assessment

Assessment
Student Recording Sheet

Use with pages 192–193 of the Student Edition

Vocabulary Review

Write the vocabulary words that match the definitions in your book.

1. _____   4. _____

2. _____   5. _____

3. _____

Understanding Key Concepts

Select the best answer from the choices given and fill in the corresponding oval.

6. Ⓐ Ⓑ Ⓒ Ⓓ   10. Ⓐ Ⓑ Ⓒ Ⓓ

7. Ⓐ Ⓑ Ⓒ Ⓓ   11. Ⓐ Ⓑ Ⓒ Ⓓ

8. Ⓐ Ⓑ Ⓒ Ⓓ   12. Ⓐ Ⓑ Ⓒ Ⓓ

9. Ⓐ Ⓑ Ⓒ Ⓓ   13. Ⓐ Ⓑ Ⓒ Ⓓ

Constructed Response

Record your answers for Questions 14–16 on a separate sheet of paper.

Thinking Critically

Record your answers for Questions 17, 19 and 20 on a separate sheet of paper.

18. **REAL WORLD BIOCHALLENGE** Follow your teacher's instructions for presenting your BioChallenge answer.

Standardized Test Practice

The Princeton Review

Part 1   Multiple Choice

Select the best answer from the choices given and fill in the corresponding oval.

21. Ⓐ Ⓑ Ⓒ Ⓓ

22. Ⓐ Ⓑ Ⓒ Ⓓ

23. Ⓐ Ⓑ Ⓒ Ⓓ

24. Ⓐ Ⓑ Ⓒ Ⓓ

25. Ⓐ Ⓑ Ⓒ Ⓓ

26. Ⓐ Ⓑ Ⓒ Ⓓ

27. Ⓐ Ⓑ Ⓒ Ⓓ

Part 2
Constructed Response/Grid In

Record your answers for Questions 28 and 29 on a separate sheet of paper.

Contents

Chapter 8 Cellular Transport and the Cell Cycle

Chapter 8

MiniLab
8.1
Cell Membrane Simulation

Formulating Models

If membranes show selective permeability, what might happen if a plastic bag (representing a cell's membrane) were filled with starch molecules on the inside and surrounded by iodine molecules on the outside?

Procedure

1 Fill a plastic bag with 50 mL of starch. Seal the bag with a twist tie.

2 Fill a beaker with 50 mL of of iodine solution. **CAUTION:** *Rinse with water if iodine gets on skin. Iodine is toxic.*

3 Note and record the color of the starch and iodine.

4 Place the bag into the beaker. **CAUTION:** *Wash your hands after handling lab materials.*

5 Note and record the color of the starch and iodine 24 hours later.

Analysis

1. Compare the color of the iodine and starch at the start and at the conclusion of the experiment.

_____

2. Which molecules crossed the membrane? What is your evidence?

_____

_____

3. Evaluate whether or not a plastic bag is an adequate model of a selectively permeable membrane.

_____

_____

_____

MiniLab 8.2 — Seeing Asters

The result of the process of mitosis is similar in plant and animal cells. However, animal cells have asters whereas plant cells do not. Animal cells undergoing mitosis clearly show these structures.

Procedure

1. Examine a slide showing fish mitosis under low- and high-power magnification. **CAUTION:** *Use care when handling prepared slides.*
2. Find cells that are undergoing mitosis. You will be able to see dark-stained rodlike structures within certain cells. These structures are chromosomes.
3. Note the appearance and location of asters. They will appear as ray or starlike structures at opposite ends of cells that are in metaphase.
4. Asters may also be observed in cells that are in other phases of the cell cycle.

Analysis

1. Describe the appearance and location of asters in cells that are in prophase.

   _____

   _____

2. Explain how you know that asters are not critical to mitosis.

   _____

   _____

3. Sketch and label a plant cell and an animal cell in prophase.

   _____

   _____

   _____

   _____

   _____

   _____

INVESTIGATE BioLab

Where is mitosis most common?

PREPARATION

Problem

Does mitosis occur at the same rate in all parts of an onion root?

Objectives

In this BioLab, you will:
- **Observe** cells in two different root areas.
- **Identify** the stages of mitosis in each area.

Materials

prepared slide of onion root tip
microscope

Skill Handbook

Use the **Skill Handbook** if you need additional help with this lab.

Safety Precautions

CAUTION: *Report any glass breakage to your teacher.*

PROCEDURE

1. Use the data table below.
2. Using Diagram **A** on page 214 of your text as a guide, locate area X on a prepared slide of onion root tip.
3. Place the prepared slide under your microscope and use low power to locate area X. **CAUTION:** *Use care when handling prepared slides.*
4. Switch to high power.
5. Using Diagram **B** on page 215 of your text as a guide:
   a. Identify those cells that are in mitosis and in interphase.
   b. Record in the data table the number of cells observed in each phase of mitosis and interphase for area X.

(NOTE: It will be easier to count and keep track of cells by following rows. See Diagram C on page 215 of your text as a guide to counting.)

6. Using Diagram **A** again, locate area Y on the same prepared slide.
7. Place the prepared slide under your microscope and use low power to locate area Y.
8. Switch to high power.
9. Using Diagram **B** as a guide:
   a. Identify those cells that are in mitosis and in interphase.
   b. Record in the data table the number of cells observed in each phase of mitosis and interphase for area Y.
10. **Cleanup and Disposal** Clean all equipment as instructed by your teacher, and return everything to its proper place.

Data Table

Phase	Area X	Area Y
Interphase		
Prophase		
Metaphase		
Anaphase		
Telophase		

Where is mitosis most common?, *continued*

Chapter **8**

ANALYZE AND CONCLUDE

1. Observing Which area of the onion root tip (X or Y) had the greatest number of cells undergoing mitosis? The fewest? Use specific totals from your data table to support your answer.

_____

_____

_____

2. Predicting If mitosis is associated with rapid growth, where do you believe is the location of most rapid root growth, area X or Y? Explain your answer.

_____

_____

_____

3. Applying Where might you look for cells in the human body that are undergoing mitosis?

_____

_____

_____

4. Critical Thinking Assume that you were not able to observe cells in every phase of mitosis. Explain why this might be, considering the length of each phase.

_____

_____

_____

5. Error Analysis What factors might cause misleading results? How could you avoid these problems?

_____

_____

_____

Chapter 8

Osmosis and the Case of the Sad Salad

Imagine opening up the refrigerator to take out carrots, lettuce, cucumbers, tomatoes, and other vegetables in order to prepare a delicious, crisp salad for your family's dinner. You rinse off the vegetables, slice them up, place them in a big bowl, and lightly season them with salt, pepper, and salad dressing. Finally, you place the bowl of salad in the refrigerator, finish some homework, and listen to a few CDs until it is time to eat. At dinner, as you prepare to enjoy your crunchy creation, you suddenly realize that your once

delicious-looking salad isn't so desirable anymore—the carrots feel like rubber coins, the cucumbers are dry and limp, and the lettuce is wilted. What has happened to your salad?

Wilting houseplants, rubbery carrots, and limp lettuce all illustrate the same important biological principle—osmosis, the diffusion of water. In this activity, you'll investigate how the process of osmosis affects plant cells, and learn some ways to prevent a sad salad.

PROCEDURE

1. Fill two 250-mL beakers three-fourths full with distilled water.

2. Add five teaspoons of table salt to one beaker, stir thoroughly, and label it "salt water." Label the other beaker "distilled water."

3. Obtain two similar carrot sticks. Tie thread or string tightly around each carrot, as shown in Figure 1. Be sure the thread is tight around each piece.

4. Submerge one carrot stick in the beaker of

salt water and the other carrot stick in the beaker of distilled water.

5. Allow the beakers to stand undisturbed for 24 hours.

6. Remove the carrot sticks. Observe the tightness of the threads. Squeeze and bend each carrot stick to determine its texture.

7. Complete the table based on your results and observations from the experiment.

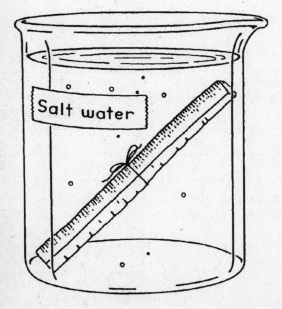

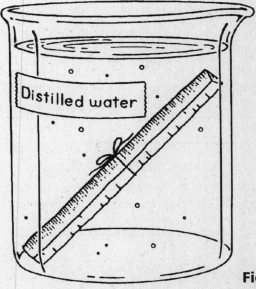

Figure 1

Chapter 8 — Osmosis and the Case of the Sad Salad

Real World BioApplications

Table 1

Condition of Carrot Stick	Type of Water
Loose thread	
Cells gained water	
Soft texture	
Tight thread	
Firm texture	
Cells lost water	

ANALYZE AND CONCLUDE

1. What was the purpose of tying thread around each carrot stick?

_____

_____

2. Using your knowledge of osmosis, draw a diagram to explain what happened to the cells of the carrot sticks in this experiment.

3. A good way to prevent a sad salad is to always keep vegetables covered with plastic wrap, rather than exposing them to the air. Use your knowledge of osmosis to explain why this method works.

_____

_____

_____

4. Supermarket workers spray fruits and vegetables with water to make them more desirable to consumers. Why does spraying vegetables with water prevent them from drying out?

_____

_____

Chapter 8

Cellular Transport and the Cell Cycle

Section 8.1 Cellular Transport

In your textbook, read about osmosis: diffusion of water.

Complete the table by checking the correct column for each statement.

Statement	Isotonic Solution	Hypotonic Solution	Hypertonic Solution
1. Causes a cell to swell			
2. Doesn't change the shape of a cell			
3. Causes osmosis			
4. Causes a cell to shrink			

In your textbook, read about passive transport and active transport.

For each item in Column A, write the letter of the matching item in Column B.

Column A	Column B

Column A

_____ **5.** Transport protein that provides a tubelike opening in the plasma membrane through which particles can diffuse

_____ **6.** Is used during active transport but not passive transport

_____ **7.** Process by which a cell takes in material by forming a vacuole around it

_____ **8.** Particle movement from an area of higher concentration to an area of lower concentration

_____ **9.** Process by which a cell expels wastes from a vacuole

_____ **10.** A form of passive transport that uses transport proteins

_____ **11.** Particle movement from an area of lower concentration to an area of higher concentration

_____ **12.** Transport protein that changes shape when a particle binds with it

Column B

a. energy

b. facilitated diffusion

c. endocytosis

d. passive transport

e. active transport

f. exocytosis

g. carrier protein

h. channel protein

Chapter 8
Cellular Transport and the Cell Cycle, continued

In your textbook, read about cell size limitations.

Determine if the statement is true. If it is not, rewrite the italicized part to make it true.

1. Most *living cells* are between 2 and 200 µm in diameter. _____

2. Diffusion of materials over long distance is *fast*. _____

3. If a cell doesn't have enough *DNA* to make all the proteins it needs, the cell cannot live.

   _____

4. As a cell's size increases, its volume increases much *slower* than its surface area.

   _____

5. If a cell's diameter doubled, the cell would require *two* times more nutrients and would have *two*

   times more wastes to excrete. _____

In your textbook, read about cell reproduction.

Use each of the terms below just once to complete the passage.

nucleus	genetic material	chromosomes	packed
identical	chromatin	vanish	cell division

The process by which two cells are produced from one cell is called **(6)** _____ .

The two cells are **(7)** _____ to the original cell. Early biologists observed that just

before cell division, several short, stringy structures appeared in the **(8)** _____ .

These structures seemed to **(9)** _____ soon after cell division. These structures,

which contain DNA and became darkly colored when stained, are now called **(10)** _____ .

Scientists eventually learned that chromosomes carry **(11)** _____ , which

is copied and passed on from generation to generation. Chromosomes normally exist as

(12) _____ , long strands of DNA wrapped around proteins. However, before

a cell divides, the chromatin becomes tightly **(13)** _____ .

Chapter 8 **Cellular Transport and the Cell Cycle,** *continued*

Section 8.2 Cell Growth and Reproduction

In your textbook, read about the cell cycle and interphase.

Complete the table by checking the correct column for each statement.

Statement	Interphase	Mitosis
14. Cell growth occurs.		
15. Nuclear division occurs.		
16. Chromosomes are distributed equally to daughter cells.		
17. Protein production is high.		
18. Chromosomes are duplicated.		
19. DNA synthesis occurs.		
20. Cytoplasm divides immediately after this period.		
21. Mitochondria and other organelles are manufactured.		

In your textbook, read about the phases of mitosis.

Identify the following phases of mitosis. Use these choices: telophase, metaphase, anaphase, prophase. Then label the diagrams. Use these choices: sister chromatids, centromere, spindle fibers, centrioles.

22. _____ **23.** _____ **24.** _____ **25.** _____

26. _____ **27.** _____ **28.** _____ **29.** _____

Answer the question.

30. How does mitosis result in tissues and organs?

_____

_____

In your textbook, read about normal control of the cell cycle and cancer.

Answer the following questions.

1. In what ways do enzymes control the cell cycle?

   _____

   _____

2. What directs the production of these enzymes?

   _____

   _____

3. What can cause the cell cycle to become uncontrolled?

   _____

   _____

   _____

   _____

4. What can result when the cell cycle becomes uncontrolled?

   _____

   _____

5. What is the relationship between environmental factors and cancer?

   _____

   _____

   _____

   _____

6. What is a tumor? Describe the final stages of cancer.

   _____

   _____

   _____

   _____

7. Cancer is the second leading cause of death in the United States. What four types of cancer are the most prevalent?

   _____

   _____

   _____

Capítulo 8

El transporte celular y el ciclo de la célula

En tu libro de texto, lee sobre la osmosis: la difusión de agua.

Completa la tabla indicando la columna correcta para cada enunciado.

Enunciado	Solución isotónica	Solución hipotónica	Solución hipertónica
1. Hace que la célula se hinche			
2. No cambia la forma de la célula			
3. Produce osmosis			
4. Hace que la célula se encoja			

En tu libro de texto, lee acerca del transporte activo y el transporte pasivo.

Anota la letra de la columna B correspondiente al enunciado de la columna A.

	Columna A	Columna B
_____	**5.** Proteína de transporte que forma una abertura tubular en la membrana plasmática, permitiendo la difusión de partículas	**a.** energía
_____	**6.** Se usa durante el transporte activo, pero no durante el transporte pasivo	**b.** difusión facilitada
_____	**7.** Proceso por el cual una célula absorbe material al formar una vacuola a su alrededor	**c.** endocitosis
_____	**8.** Movimiento de partículas desde una zona de alta concentración hacia una zona de baja concentración	**d.** transporte pasivo
_____	**9.** Proceso por el cual una la célula excreta desechos desde una vacuola	**e.** transporte activo
_____	**10.** Forma de transporte pasivo que usa proteínas de transporte	**f.** exocitosis
_____	**11.** Movimiento de partículas desde un área de baja concentración hacia un área de alta concentración	**g.** proteína transportadora
_____	**12.** Proteína de transporte que cambia de forma cuando se une con una partícula	**h.** proteína de canal

El transporte celular y el ciclo de la célula, *continuación*

Sección 8.2 Crecimiento y reproducción celulares

En tu libro de texto, lee acerca de las limitaciones en el tamaño de las células.

Si el enunciado es verdadero, escribe *verdadero*; de lo contrario, modifica la sección en itálicas para hacer verdadero el enunciado.

1. La mayoría de las *células vivas* tienen un diámetro entre 2 y 200 µm. _____

2. La difusión de partículas a larga distancia ocurre *rápidamente*. _____

3. Si una célula no tiene el suficiente *DNA* para fabricar todas las proteínas que necesita, se muere.

_____

4. Conforme aumenta el tamaño de una célula, su volumen aumenta más *lentamente* que el área de su

superficie.

_____

5. Si duplica su diámetro, una célula requerirá el *doble* de nutrientes y eliminará el *doble* de desechos.

_____

En tu libro de texto, lee sobre la reproducción celular.

Usa cada término una sola vez para completar el párrafo.

núcleo	material genético	cromosomas	condensa
idénticas	cromatina	desvanecerse	división celular

El proceso en que se producen dos células a partir de una sola célula, se conoce como

(6) _____ . Las dos células son **(7)** _____ a la célula

original. Los primeros biólogos observaron que justo antes de la división celular, aparecían varias estruc-

turas fibrosas y cortas en el **(8)** _____ . Estas estructuras que parecen **(9)**

_____ poco después de la división celular, que contienen DNA y que se tiñen

de color oscuro, ahora se conocen como **(10)** _____ . Los científicos des-

cubrieron después que los cromosomas contienen **(11)** _____ , el cual se copia

y se transmite de generación en generación. Los cromosomas normalmente existen como

(12) _____ , largas fibras de DNA enrolladas alrededor de proteínas. Sin

embargo, antes de que la célula se divida, la cromatina se **(13)** _____ .

Capítulo 8

El transporte celular y el ciclo de la célula, *continuación*

Sección 8.2 Crecimiento y reproducción celulares

En tu libro de texto, lee sobre el ciclo celular y la interfase.

Completa la tabla indicando la columna correspondiente a cada enunciado.

Enunciado	Interfase	Mitosis
14. La célula crece.		
15. El núcleo se divide.		
16. Los cromosomas se distribuyen equitativamente a cada célula hija.		
17. Aumenta la producción de proteínas.		
18. Se duplican los cromosomas.		
19. Se sintetiza DNA.		
20. El citoplasma se divide inmediatamente después de este período.		
21. Se fabrican mitocondrias y otros organelos.		

En tu libro de texto, lee sobre las fases de la mitosis.

Identifica las fases de la mitosis. Usa las siguientes opciones: telofase, metafase, anafase y profase. Después, identifica las estructuras señaladas en los diagramas. Usa las siguientes opciones: cromátides hermanas, centrómero, fibras del huso y centriolos.

22. _____ **23.** _____ **24.** _____ **25.** _____

26. _____ **27.** _____ **28.** _____ **29.** _____

Contesta la pregunta.

30. ¿Por qué la mitosis ayuda en la formación de tejidos y órganos?

_____

_____

_____

En tu libro de texto, lee sobre el control normal del ciclo celular y el cáncer.

Responde las siguientes preguntas.

1. ¿Cómo controlan las enzimas el ciclo celular?

2. ¿Qué dirige la producción de estas enzimas?

3. ¿Qué factores pueden ocasionar la pérdida de control del ciclo celular?

4. ¿Qué consecuencias puede acarrear la pérdida de control del ciclo celular?

5. ¿Qué relación hay entre los factores ambientales y el cáncer?

6. ¿Qué es un tumor? Describe las etapa finales de un cáncer.

7. El cáncer es la segunda causa de mortalidad en los Estados Unidos. ¿Cuáles son los cuatro tipos de cáncer de mayor incidencia?

Chapter 8

Cellular Transport and the Cell Cycle

Concept Mapping

Use with Chapter 8, Section 8.1

Transport Through Membranes

Complete the concept map on transport of materials through membranes. Use these words or phrases one or more times: *simple diffusion, energy, higher concentration, lower concentration, osmosis, passive, facilitated diffusion.*

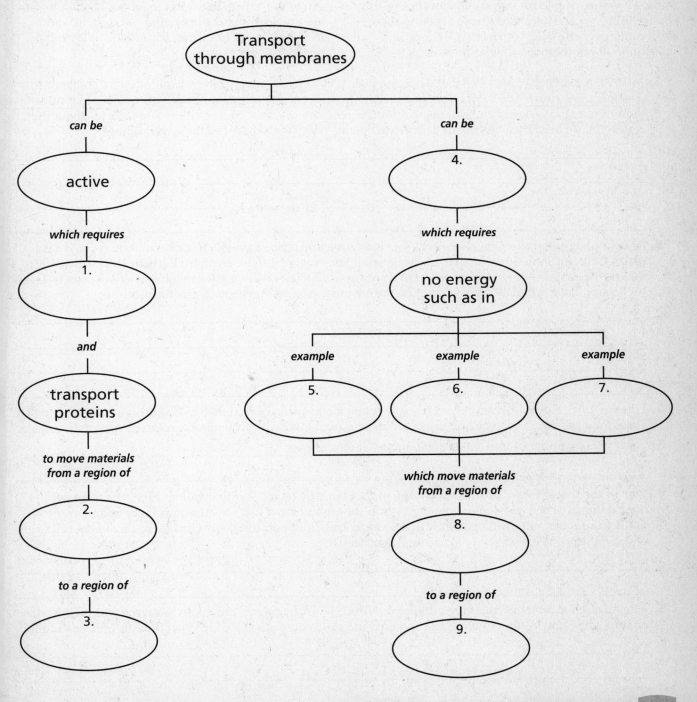

Chapter 8 Cellular Transport and the Cell Cycle

Use with Chapter 8, Section 8.3

Linking a Tumor Suppressor Gene to the Cell Cycle

Individuals with close relatives who have certain types of cancers are often considered at higher risk for these cancers than other members of the population. However, people with no family history can also suffer from cancer. Researchers have begun to identify certain genetic defects that may predispose a person to develop cancer. One of these defects involves a human gene known as p53. The p53 gene is called a *tumor suppressor* because, when it operates normally, it appears to prevent the uncontrolled growth of cells. To learn more about how biologists are investigating the operation of this gene and its possible link to cancer, answer the following questions.

1. In 1990, researchers discovered that defects in gene p53 were common to a few families with a tendency to develop a rare, inherited form of breast cancer and some cancers of the bone and soft tissues. The study did not attempt to determine whether or not the gene defects cause cancer. Some news stories about the research were headlined "Breast Cancer Gene Found." Why were these headlines misleading?

_____

_____

_____

_____

2. As cells undergo mitosis, mistakes in DNA replication and changes in DNA, called mutations, may take place. Cells are sometimes capable of recognizing and reversing these changes. Early in 1993, researchers discovered that p53 may be involved in preventing a cell from dividing after mutations or mistakes in DNA replication have occurred. What might be the adaptive value of a gene with this function?

_____

_____

_____

_____

3. Later in 1993, three different research teams simultaneously discovered that p53 controls a second gene that codes for a protein causing cells to remain in interphase. How does this finding tie in to the previous studies?

_____

_____

4. One of the three research teams was trying to find out why old cells stop dividing. First, the team developed cultures of actively dividing young cells in the laboratory. Then they inserted short fragments of DNA from older, nondividing cells into the young cells and monitored any changes in the young cells' rate of cell division. What was the researchers' hypothesis?

_____

_____

5. The research team found that three different old-cell DNA fragments caused division of young cells to slow or stop. Only one of these fragments contained the gene controlled by p53. What does this finding imply?

_____

_____

Master 18

Water in the Cell

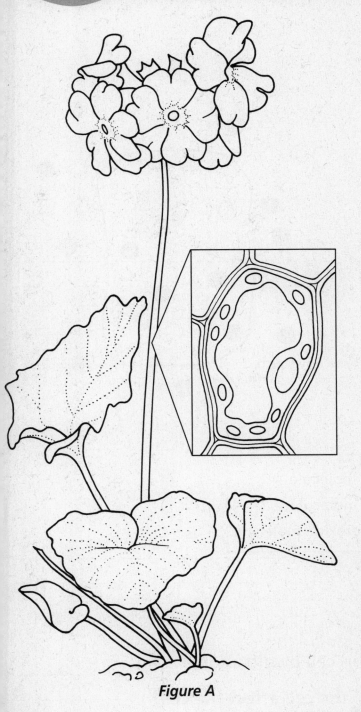

Figure A

Figure B

1 How do the plant cells in figures A and B differ?

2 What is the effect of this difference on the plants?

Master 19

Diffusion and Cell Size

Use with Chapter 8, Section 8.2

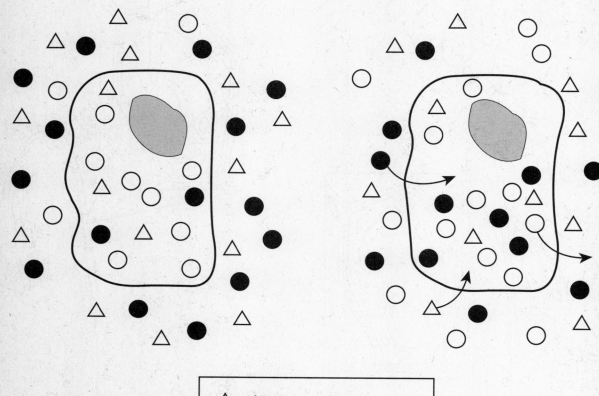

△ Glucose molecule
● Oxygen molecule
○ Carbon dioxide molecule

❶ What materials move through this cell by diffusion?

❷ How might increasing the size of the cell affect the cell?

Master 20 **Uncontrolled Cell Division**

❶ The weeds in this garden are spreading rapidly. What effect might this have on the flowers in the garden?

❷ Suppose a change in a cell's genes causes the cell to reproduce very rapidly. How might this increased rate of reproduction affect surrounding cells?

Master 8

Osmosis

Before osmosis   After osmosis

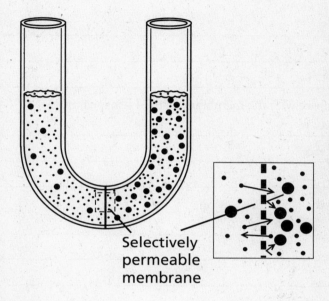
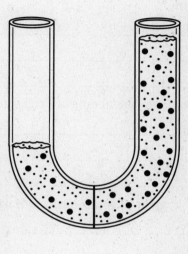

Selectively permeable membrane

- Water molecule
- Sugar molecule

Cell in Isotonic Solution	Cell in Hypotonic Solution	Cell in Hypertonic Solution

Water molecules
Dissolved particles

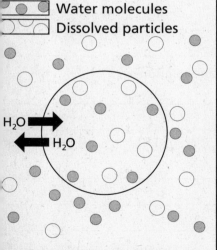
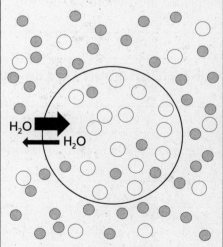
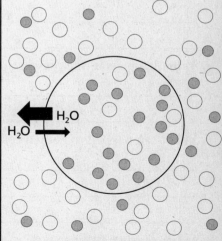

▲ In an isotonic solution, water molecules move into and out of the cell at the same rate.

▲ In a hypotonic solution, water enters a cell by osmosis, causing the cell to swell.

▲ In a hypertonic solution, water leaves a cell by osmosis, causing the cell to shrink.

Worksheet
8 **Osmosis**

1. Look at the U-shaped tube at the top of the transparency. Why did the number of water molecules on each side of the membrane change, whereas the number of sugar molecules stayed the same?

_____

_____

_____

2. How does the plasma membrane of a cell compare with the membrane in the U-shaped tube?

_____

_____

_____

3. Explain the behavior of water molecules in the isotonic solution.

_____

_____

_____

4. Does osmosis occur if a cell is placed in an isotonic solution?

_____

_____

5. Why does water enter a cell that is placed in a hypotonic solution?

_____

_____

6. What happens to the pressure inside a cell that is placed in a hypertonic solution?

_____

_____

7. What can happen to animal cells when placed in a hypotonic solution? Explain.

_____

_____

_____

8. What causes a plant to wilt?

_____

_____

_____

Master
9

Active Transport

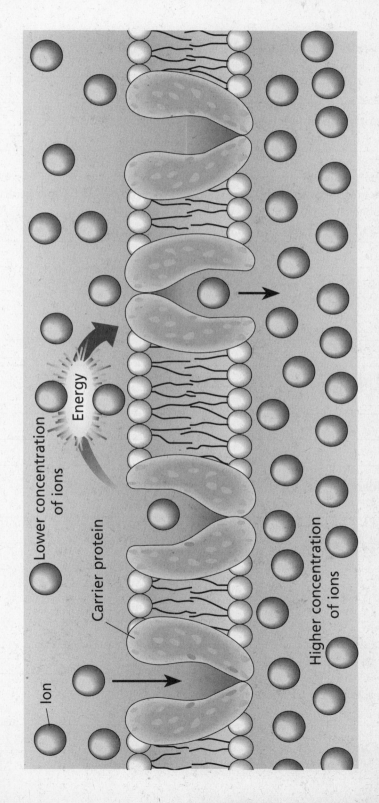

Lower concentration of ions

Energy

Carrier protein

Ion

Higher concentration of ions

Worksheet 9 — Active Transport

1. Which type of transport protein is involved in active transport?

_____

_____

2. Describe the concentration gradient shown in the transparency.

_____

_____

3. Why must cells use energy to move particles from a region of lower concentration to a region of higher concentration?

_____

_____

4. Describe the process of active transport.

_____

_____

_____

5. What is the source of the energy used in active transport?

_____

_____

_____

6. How does endocytosis differ from the process shown in the transparency?

_____

_____

_____

7. Why is endocytosis considered a type of active transport?

_____

_____

_____

8. What process of active transport is the reverse of endocytosis? Explain

_____

_____

Master
10   **Mitosis**

Prophase

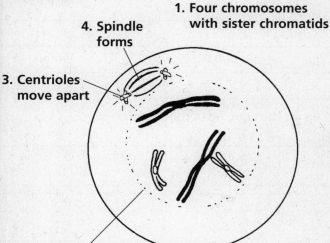

1. Four chromosomes with sister chromatids
4. Spindle forms
3. Centrioles move apart
2. Disappearing nuclear envelope

Metaphase

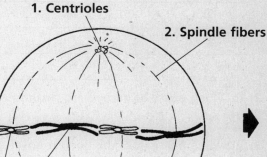

1. Centrioles
2. Spindle fibers
3. Chromosomes at equator of spindle

Anaphase

1. Each chromatid is a copy of one original chromosome
2. Spindle fibers move chromatids toward centrioles

Telophase

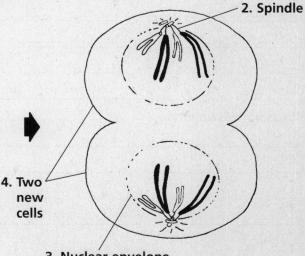

1. Four chromosomes in each cell
2. Spindle
4. Two new cells
3. Nuclear envelope reforms

Worksheet
10 **Mitosis**

1. When and how is the spindle formed?

_____

_____

_____

2. In which phase of mitosis are chromosomes lined up on the equator of the spindle?

_____

3. In which phase does the nuclear envelope disappear?

_____

4. Which phase of the cell cycle follows mitosis?

_____

5. Are the cells shown in the transparency those of animals or plants? Explain your answer.

_____

_____

_____

6. What is cytokinesis? How does it differ in animal cells and plant cells?

_____

_____

_____

_____

_____

7. Why is mitosis important?

_____

_____

_____

_____

Master
11

Active Versus
Passive Transport

Passive Transport

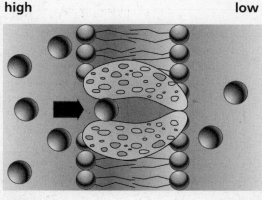

high   low

outside cell   inside cell

high   low

outside cell   inside cell

Active Transport

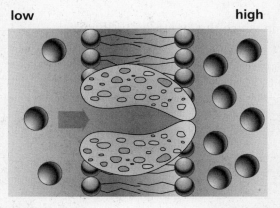

low   high

outside cell   inside cell

Energy to transport substance

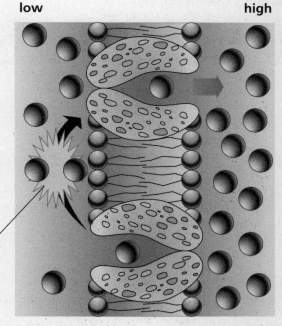

low   high

outside cell   inside cell

Worksheet 11 Active Versus Passive Transport

1. Some people describe diffusion as the process by which "something moves from where it is to where it is not." Explain why this description is accurate and why it is not.

_____

_____

2. Explain what is meant by *concentration gradient*.

_____

_____

A.	
Concentration Gradient of Molecules	
Outside the cell	Inside the cell
B.	

The model above represents a cell in a solution. Use it to answer questions 3 and 4.

3. In space A, draw an arrow that shows the direction in which the molecules will move during passive transport.

4. In space B, draw an arrow that shows the direction in which the molecules will move during active transport.

5. What type of passive transport is shown in the transparency? Explain.

_____

_____

6. Why is passive transport called *passive*?

_____

_____

7. In the illustration of active transport, why is energy needed to move the particles across the plasma membrane?

_____

_____

8. Describe the role of carrier proteins during active transport.

_____

_____

Master 12

Osmosis and Hypotonic, Hypertonic, and Isotonic Solutions

Hypotonic Solution

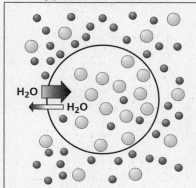

Approximate ratio of water molecules to dissolved particles

Inside cell:

__1__ water molecules: __3__ dissolved particles

Outside cell:

__4__ water molecules: __1__ dissolved particles

Hypertonic Solution

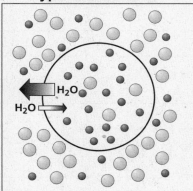

Approximate ratio of water molecules to dissolved particles

Inside cell:

__5.5__ water molecules: __1__ dissolved particles

Outside cell:

__1__ water molecules: __2.5__ dissolved particles

Isotonic Solution

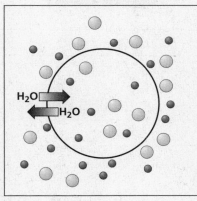

Approximate ratio of water molecules to dissolved particles

Inside cell:

__1__ water molecules: __1__ dissolved particles

Outside cell:

__1__ water molecules: __1__ dissolved particles

● **Water molecules**

○ **Dissolved particles**

Count the water molecules and dissolved particles inside and outside each cell.

Worksheet 12 — Osmosis and Hypotonic, Hypertonic, and Isotonic Solutions

Reteaching Skills

Use with Chapter 8, Section 8.1

1. Define the following terms:

a. osmosis

_____

_____

b. hypotonic solution

_____

_____

c. hypertonic solution

_____

_____

d. isotonic solution

_____

_____

2. When a cell is in a hypotonic solution, how will water molecules move?

_____

_____

3. When a cell is in a hypertonic solution, how will water molecules move?

_____

_____

4. When a cell is in an isotonic solution, how will water molecules move?

_____

_____

5. Explain how hypotonic and hypertonic solutions can make a plant rigid and firm or make it wilt.

_____

_____

6. Osmosis is a form of passive transport. Explain how facilitated diffusion, which is another form of passive transport, is different from osmosis.

_____

_____

_____

Master 13 Cell Cycle

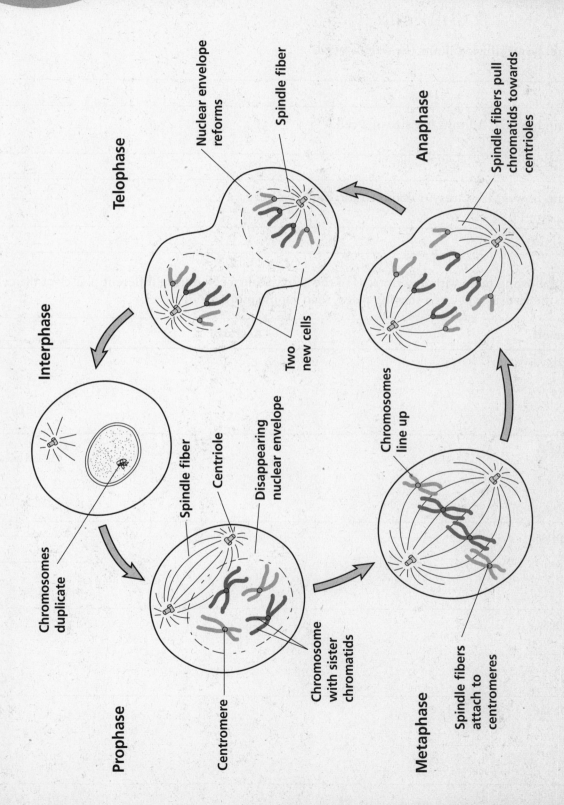

Telophase — Nuclear envelope reforms — Spindle fiber

Anaphase — Spindle fibers pull chromatids towards centrioles

Interphase — Chromosomes duplicate

Two new cells

Prophase — Spindle fiber — Centriole — Disappearing nuclear envelope — Chromosome with sister chromatids — Centromere

Metaphase — Chromosomes line up — Spindle fibers attach to centromeres

Worksheet 13 · Cell Cycle

1. Explain how diffusion limits the size of a cell.

_____

_____

2. Explain how DNA limits the size of a cell.

_____

_____

3. Explain how surface area-to-volume ratio limits cell size.

_____

_____

Fill in the following table with descriptions of the activities in a cell during different phases of the cell cycle. Use the transparency as a starting place, then supply more details.

Time Period	Activity
4. Interphase	
5. Prophase	
6. Metaphase	
7. Anaphase	
8. Telophase	

Chapter 8 Cellular Transport and the Cell Cycle

Reviewing Vocabulary

Write the word or phrase that best completes each statement.

1. The transport of materials against a concentration gradient is called _____ .

2. The phase of mitosis in which the sister chromatids separate from each other is _____ .

3. A solution in which the concentration of dissolved substances is lower than the concentration inside a cell is _____ .

4. The sequence of growth and division of a cell make up the _____ .

5. The period during which chromosomes duplicate is _____ .

6. The segment of DNA that controls the production of a protein is a _____ .

7. The phase of mitosis in which chromosomes line up on the equator of the spindle is _____ .

8. The two halves of a doubled chromosome structure are called _____ .

9. The uncontrolled division of cells may result in _____ .

10. Passive transport with the aid of transport proteins is _____ .

11. The process by which nuclear material is divided equally between two new cells is _____ .

12. Some cells surround and take in materials by the process of _____ .

13. The structures that hold together sister chromatids are _____ .

Write a sentence that uses each pair of terms.

14. (spindle, centrioles)

_____

_____

15. (tissues, organs)

_____

_____

Understanding Main Ideas (Part A)

In the space at the left, write the letter of the word or phrase that best completes the statement or answers the question.

_____ **1.** When placed in a hypotonic solution, a cell will
   a. diffuse.   **b.** shrink.   **c.** swell.   **d.** stay the same.

_____ **2.** As the size of a cell increases,
   a. volume increases faster than surface area.
   b. volume increases and surface area decreases.
   c. volume and surface area increase at the same rate.
   d. surface area increases faster than volume.

_____ **3.** The longest phase of the cell cycle is
   a. prophase.   **b.** interphase.   **c.** metaphase.   **d.** mitosis.

_____ **4.** Which of the following does *not* control the cell cycle?
   a. DNA   **b.** mitosis   **c.** enzymes   **d.** genes

_____ **5.** Tangled strands of DNA wrapped around protein molecules make up the
   a. spindle.   **b.** microtubules.   **c.** nuclear envelope.   **d.** chromatin.

_____ **6.** By the end of prophase, each of the following has occurred *except*
   a. chromatin coiling into visible chromosomes.
   b. breaking down of the nuclear envelope.
   c. forming of the spindle.
   d. lining up of chromosomes in the cell.

_____ **7.** Each of the following is an example of passive transport *except*
   a. diffusion.   **b.** osmosis.
   c. exocytosis.   **d.** facilitated diffusion.

_____ **8.** The cells that make up a tissue
   a. are different.   **b.** are the result of interphase.
   c. have the same function.   **d.** no longer undergo mitosis.

_____ **9.** Each of the following is a cause of some cancers *except*
   a. damaged genes.   **b.** bacteria.
   c. ultraviolet radiation.   **d.** viruses.

_____ **10.** Among the following, the term that includes all of the others is
   a. interphase.   **b.** nuclear division. **c.** mitosis.   **d.** cell cycle.

Cellular Transport and the Cell Cycle, *continued*

Understanding Main Ideas (Part B)

The diagrams below show six cells in various phases of the cell cycle, labeled A through F. Use the diagrams to answer questions 1–7.

Phases of the Cell Cycle

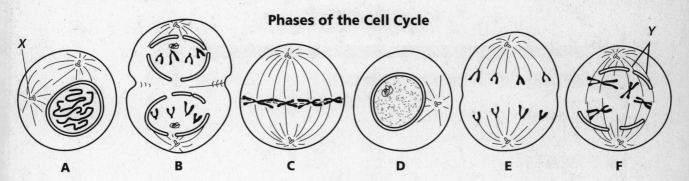

A   B   C   D   E   F

1. Which cell is in metaphase? _____

2. Cells A and F show an early and a late stage of the same phase of mitosis. What phase is it?
_____

3. In cell A, what structure is labeled X?
_____

4. In cell F, what structure is labeled Y?
_____

5. Which cell is not in a phase of mitosis?
_____

6. What two main changes are taking place in cell B?
_____
_____

7. Sequence the six diagrams in order from first to last.
_____

Answer the following question.

8. What are the main differences between cytokinesis in plant cells and in animal cells?
_____
_____
_____
_____

Chapter 8 Cellular Transport and the Cell Cycle, *continued*

Thinking Critically

The graph shows typical concentrations of several ions inside and outside an animal cell. Concentrations of ions inside the cell are shown in gray, outside in black. Use the graph to answer questions 1–5.

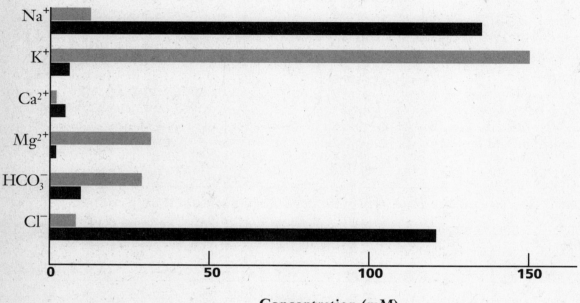

Concentration (mM)

1. Compared to its surroundings, does an animal cell contain a higher or lower concentration of potassium (K^+) ions? _____

2. Which ions are in the greatest concentration outside the animal cell? _____

3. Which ions are in the lowest concentration inside the animal cell? _____

4. What is the approximate concentration, in mM, of Mg^{2+} ions inside the cell? _____

5. If all available Na^+ and Cl^- ions combine to form NaCl, do any excess Na^+ or Cl^- ions remain? If so, which? _____

Answer the following question.

6. Describe the process by which a cell maintains differences in concentrations of certain ions on either side of the plasma membrane.

_____

_____

_____

_____

Chapter 8 Cellular Transport and the Cell Cycle, *continued*

Applying Scientific Methods

The large size of many fruits and flowers is the result of polyploidy, a condition in which the nuclei of an organism's cells contain extra sets of chromosomes. Polyploidy often occurs naturally, but it can also be artificially induced by plant breeders. How have breeders been able to mimic a naturally occurring phenomenon?

Researchers have determined that the chemical colchicine suppresses cell division by preventing the formation of spindle fibers. Without these fibers, the sister chromatids cannot become properly oriented for separation into individual nuclei. In effect, mitosis is stopped after prophase. However, the cell may continue to make copies of its chromosomes. As a result, the nucleus of the cell contains multiple sets of chromosomes.

Suppose a researcher wished to investigate how extra sets of chromosomes are produced. First, she treated two onion roots with a colchicine solution and left two roots untreated. After a period of several days, she placed thin slices from each root tip on separate microscope slides, stained the specimens, and examined the slides under a microscope at high power.

1. What is the hypothesis the researcher investigated?

_____

_____

2. Which root tips were the control group? Which root tips were the experimental group?

_____

_____

3. What was the independent variable in the investigation?

_____

_____

4. What was the dependent variable?

_____

_____

5. How do you predict the slides of treated and untreated root tips will differ?

_____

_____

_____

6. If the researcher finds only cells in interphase and prophase on the slides of treated root tips but not on the slides of untreated root tips, what might be her interpretation?

_____

_____

Applying Scientific Methods *continued*

7. What results might lead the researcher to conclude that the colchicine had no effect on the onion cells?

_____

_____

_____

_____

8. "How does treating cells with colchicine prevent the formation of spindle fibers?" Is this question the statement of the problem or the conclusion of a further investigation? Explain.

_____

_____

9. How might the researcher proceed to find out how treating cells with colchicine prevents the formation of spindle fibers?

_____

_____

_____

_____

10. Why does polyploidy result in larger fruits and flowers?

_____

_____

_____

_____

_____

Chapter 8 Assessment
Student Recording Sheet

Use with pages 218–219 of the Student Edition

Vocabulary Review

Write *true* if the statement is true. If the statement is false, write the vocabulary word that makes the sentence true.

1. _____
2. _____
3. _____
4. _____
5. _____

Understanding Key Concepts

Select the best answer from the choices given and fill in the corresponding oval.

6. Ⓐ Ⓑ Ⓒ Ⓓ
7. Ⓐ Ⓑ Ⓒ Ⓓ
8. Ⓐ Ⓑ Ⓒ Ⓓ
9. Ⓐ Ⓑ Ⓒ Ⓓ
10. Ⓐ Ⓑ Ⓒ Ⓓ
11. Ⓐ Ⓑ Ⓒ Ⓓ
12. Ⓐ Ⓑ Ⓒ Ⓓ
13. Ⓐ Ⓑ Ⓒ Ⓓ

Constructed Response

Record your answers for Questions 14–16 on a separate sheet of paper.

Thinking Critically

Record your answer for Question 17 on a separate sheet of paper.

18. **REAL WORLD BIOCHALLENGE** Follow your teacher's instructions for presenting your BioChallenge answer.

Standardized Test Practice

Part 1   Multiple Choice

Select the best answer from the choices given and fill in the corresponding oval.

19. Ⓐ Ⓑ Ⓒ Ⓓ
20. Ⓐ Ⓑ Ⓒ Ⓓ
21. Ⓐ Ⓑ Ⓒ Ⓓ
22. Ⓐ Ⓑ Ⓒ Ⓓ
23. Ⓐ Ⓑ Ⓒ Ⓓ
24. Ⓐ Ⓑ Ⓒ Ⓓ
25. Ⓐ Ⓑ Ⓒ Ⓓ
26. Ⓐ Ⓑ Ⓒ Ⓓ

Part 2
Constructed Response/Grid In

Record your answers for Questions 27 and 28 on a separate sheet of paper.

Chapter 9 Energy in a Cell

BioDigest 3 The Life of a Cell

Chapter 9

MiniLab 9.1

Experiment

Separating Pigments

Chromatography is an important diagnostic tool. In this experiment, you will use paper chromatography to separate different pigments from plant leaves.

Procedure 👓 🧤 🧫

1. Obtain a pre-made plant solution from your teacher.
2. Place a few drops 2 cm high on a 5-cm × 14-cm strip of filter paper. Let it dry. Make sure a small colored spot is visible.
3. Pour rubbing alcohol in a 100-mL beaker to a depth of 1 cm.
4. Place the filter paper into the beaker. The filter paper should touch the alcohol, but the dot should not. Hold it in place 15 minutes and observe what happens.

Analysis

1. **Explain** What did you observe as the solvent moved up the filter paper?

_____

_____

2. **Infer** Why did you see different colors at different locations on the filter paper?

_____

_____

MiniLab 9.2

Formulating Models

Use Isotopes to Understand Photosynthesis

C. B. van Niel demonstrated that photosynthesis is a light-dependent reaction in which the O_2 comes from water. Other scientists confirmed his findings by using radioactive isotopes of oxygen as tracers. Radioactive tracers are used to follow a particular molecule through a chemical reaction.

Procedure 👓

1 Study the following general equation that resulted from the van Niel experiment:

$$CO_2 + 2H_2O^* \rightarrow CH_2O + H_2O + O_2^*$$

2 Radioactive water, water tagged with an isotope of oxygen as a tracer (shown by the *), was used. Note where the tagged oxygen ends up on the right side of the equation.

3 Assume that the experiment was repeated, but this time a radioactive tag was put on the oxygen in CO_2.

4 Using materials provided by your teacher, model what you predict the appearance of the results would be. Your model must include a "tag" to indicate the oxygen isotope on the left side of the arrow as well as where it ends up on the right side of the arrow.

5 You also must use labels or different colors in your model to indicate what happens to the carbon and hydrogen.

Analysis

1. Explain How can an isotope be used as a tag?

_____

_____

2. Use Models Using your model, predict what happens to:
   a. all oxygen molecules that originated from carbon dioxide.

_____

_____

   b. all carbon molecules that originated from carbon dioxide.

_____

_____

   c. all hydrogen molecules that originated from water.

_____

_____

MiniLab 9.3 — Determine if Apple Juice Ferments

Predicting

Organisms such as yeast have the ability to break down food molecules and synthesize ATP when no oxygen is available. When the appropriate food is available, yeast can carry out alcoholic fermentation, producing CO_2. Thus, the production of CO_2 can be used to judge whether alcoholic fermentation is taking place.

Procedure

1. Carefully study the diagram on page 236 of your text and set up the experiment as shown.
2. Hold the test tube in a beaker of warm (not hot) water and observe.

Analysis

1. What were the gas bubbles that came from the plastic pipette?

_____

_____

2. Predict what would happen to the rate of bubbles given off if more yeast were present in the mixture.

_____

_____

3. Why was the test tube placed in warm water?

_____

_____

4. On the basis of your observations, was this process aerobic or anaerobic? Explain.

_____

_____

What factors influence photosynthesis?

Chapter 9

PREPARATION

Problem
How do different wavelengths of light a plant receives affect its rate of photosynthesis?

Objectives
In this BioLab, you will:
- **Observe** photosynthesis in an aquatic organism.
- **Measure** the rate of photosynthesis.
- **Research** the wavelengths of various colors of light.
- **Observe** how various wavelengths of light influence the rate of photosynthesis.
- **Use the Internet** to collect and compare data from other students.

Materials
1000-mL beaker

three *Elodea* plants
string
washers
colored cellophane, assorted colors
lamp with reflector and 150-watt bulb
0.25 percent sodium hydrogen carbonate (baking soda) solution
watch with second hand

Safety Precautions 🔲 👓 🧤 🧪
Always wear goggles in the lab.

Skill Handbook
Use the **Skill Handbook** if you need additional help with this lab.

PROCEDURE

---

1. Construct a basic setup like the one shown on page 238 of your text.
2. Use the data table below to record your measurements. Be sure to include a column for each color of light you will investigate and a column for the control experiment.
3. Place the *Elodea* plants in the beaker, then completely cover the plants with water. Add some of the baking soda solution. The solution provides CO_2 for the aquarium plants. **Be sure to use the same amount of water and solution for each trial.**
4. Conduct a control experiment by directing the lamp (without colored cellophane) on the

plant and notice when you see the bubbles.
5. Observe and record the number of oxygen bubbles that *Elodea* generates in five minutes.
6. Repeat steps 4 and 5 with a piece of colored cellophane. Record your observations.
7. Repeat steps 4 and 5 with a different color of cellophane and record your observations.
8. Go to **bdol.glencoe.com/internet_lab** to **post your data.**
9. **Cleanup and Disposal** Return plant material to an aquarium to prevent it from drying out.

Data Table

	Control	Color 1	Color 2
Bubbles observed in five minutes			

INTERNET
BioLab **What factors influence photosynthesis?,** *continued*

ANALYZE AND CONCLUDE

1. Interpreting Observations From where did the bubbles of oxygen emerge? Why?

_____

_____

2. Making Inferences Explain how counting bubbles measures the rate of photosynthesis.

_____

_____

_____

3. Using the Internet Look up the wavelengths of the colors of light you used. Make a graph of your data and data posted by other students with the rate of photosynthesis per minute plotted against the wavelength of light you tested for both the control and experimental setups. Write a sentence or two explaining the graph.

_____

_____

_____

_____

4. Error Analysis Why was it important to use the same amount of sodium hydrogen carbonate in each trial?

_____

_____

_____

Chapter 9 Bioluminescence and Behavior

You've probably enjoyed the blinking lights of fireflies on a summer evening. But fireflies are not the only species that can glow in the dark. More than 40 orders of animals include species that produce light. Many plants, fungi, and bacteria can glow on their own, too. The process by which organisms produce light is called bioluminescence.

People study bioluminescent organisms for a variety of reasons. Marine biologists might study bioluminescent species to understand evolutionary relationships among marine animals. Medical researchers have developed methods of using bioluminescent organisms and the luminous materials they produce as screening techniques for a variety of medical conditions, such as thyroid disease. Environmental technologists are developing techniques for using bioluminescent bacteria as a means of detecting organic pollutants in lakes and rivers.

In this activity, you'll explore the chemistry of bioluminescence, and then design an experiment to test a hypothesis about bioluminescence and animal behavior.

Part A: Producing Light

Researchers interested in bioluminescence conducted a series of experiments to study several species that were able to produce their own light. The notebook in Figure 1 shows the conclusions the researchers formed in four of the experiments.

Experiment 1: All bioluminescent organisms contain two substances: luciferin and an enzyme called luciferase. Bioluminescence will occur only if both are present.	**Experiment 3:** The color of light produced varies among species and from one individual to another within species.
Experiment 2: The exact chemical composition of luciferin and luciferase may vary from one species to another.	**Experiment 4:** Bioluminescence will not occur in the absence of oxygen.

Figure 1

1. Based on the information in the notebook, what are three essential components of bioluminescence?

_____

_____

2. Based on the information, what is one hypothesis you might make concerning the cause of the variance in the color of light produced?

_____

_____

As the researchers worked, it became clear that another substance might be essential for the chemical reaction that produces bioluminescent light. Figure 2 shows data collected in a fifth experiment in which the scientist explored the role of ATP. (ATP, adenosine triphosphate, is a component of DNA. As such, it is present in every cell of every living organism. ATP supplies the energy needed for many metabolic processes.)

Chapter 9 Bioluminescence and Behavior

3. From this data, what conclusion can you draw about the role of ATP in bioluminescence?

_____

_____

_____

_____

Figure 2

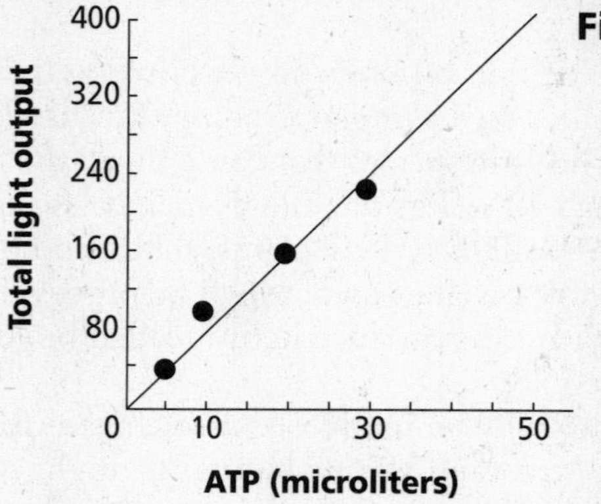

[Graph: x-axis labeled "ATP (microliters)" with values 0, 10, 30, 50; y-axis labeled "Total light output" with values 80, 160, 240, 320, 400; data points forming a roughly linear relationship]

4. The word equation below shows the products formed during the chemical reaction that produces bioluminescence. Use the information from the five experiments to complete the word equation.

luciferin	+ _____	+ _____	+ _____	=
oxidized luciferin	+ AMP (adenosine monophosphate)	+ PP (pyrophosphate)	+ water	+ light

Part B: Using Light

All organisms produce bioluminescent light by a similar chemical reaction. But the role of bioluminescence in the adaptive behavior of different species varies. Look at the data collected in Figure 3 about three different bioluminescent marine organisms.

Figure 3

Lantern fish	**Deep-sea squid**	**Colobonema**
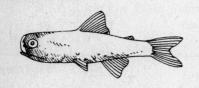	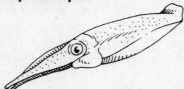	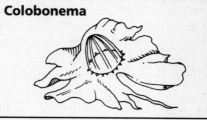
• Pattern of distribution of light organs is different for each species. • Males have patterns that differ from those of females within the same species.	• Can shoot out a luminescent cloud from rear. • Clouds appear to be related to the presence of potential predators.	• Lives in upper areas of water where light intensity varies. • Can break off brightly colored tentacles.

1. Choose one organism from the data table in Figure 3. Suggest a testable hypothesis explaining the use of bioluminescence by that organism.

_____

_____

2. How could you test your hypothesis? What information would you want to gather?

_____

_____

3. Write an experimental procedure on another sheet of paper.

Chapter
9 Energy in a Cell

In your textbook, read about cell energy.

Use each of the terms below just once to complete the passage.

energy	phosphate	adenine	charged
ATP	chemical bonds	work	ribose

To do biological **(1)** _____ , cells require energy. A quick source

of energy that cells use is the molecule **(2)** _____ . The **(3)** _____

in this molecule is stored in its **(4)** _____ . ATP is composed of a(n)

(5) _____ molecule bonded to a(n) **(6)** _____ sugar.

Three **(7)** _____ molecules called **(8)** _____ groups

are attached to the sugar.

In your textbook, read about forming and breaking down ATP and the uses of cell energy.

Examine the diagram below. Then answer the questions.

9. How is energy stored and released by ATP?

_____

_____

_____

_____

10. How do cells use the energy released from ATP?

_____

_____

_____

Chapter 9 **Energy in a Cell,** *continued*

Section 9.2 Photosynthesis: Trapping the Sun's Energy

In your textbook, read about trapping the sun's energy.

Determine if the statement is true. If it is not, rewrite the italicized part to make it true.

1. Photosynthesis is the process plants use to trap the sun's energy to make *glucose*.

_____

2. ATP molecules are made during the *light-independent* reactions of photosynthesis.

_____

3. *Carbon dioxide* gas is produced during photosynthesis.

_____

4. The light-dependent reactions of photosynthesis take place in the membranes of the thylakoid discs in *mitochondria*.

_____

5. The thylakoid membranes contain chlorophyll and other pigments that *absorb* sunlight.

_____

In your textbook, read about the light-dependent reactions of photosynthesis.

Number the following steps of the light-dependent reactions in the order in which they occur.

_____ **6.** The energy lost by electrons as they pass through the electron transport chain is used to make ATP.

_____ **7.** The electrons pass from the chlorophyll to an electron transport chain.

_____ **8.** Sunlight strikes the chlorophyll molecules in the thylakoid membranes.

_____ **9.** NADP⁺ molecules change to NADPH as they carry the electrons to the stroma of the chloroplast.

_____ **10.** The sunlight's energy is transferred to the chlorophyll's electrons.

_____ **11.** The electrons are passed down a second electron transport chain.

Answer the following questions.

12. How are the electrons that are lost by the chlorophyll molecules replaced?

_____

_____

13. How do plants produce oxygen during photosynthesis?

_____

_____

Chapter 9 **Energy in a Cell,** *continued*

Reinforcement and Study Guide

Section 9.2 Photosynthesis: Trapping the Sun's Energy

In your textbook, read about the light-independent reactions.

Circle the letter of the choice that best completes the statement or answers the question.

14. The Calvin cycle includes
    a. the light-dependent reactions.   **b.** an electron transport chain.
    c. the light-independent reactions.   **d.** photolysis.

15. The Calvin cycle takes place in the
    a. mitochondria.   **b.** stroma.
    c. nucleus.   **c.** thylakoid membrane.

16. What product of the light-dependent reactions is used in the Calvin cycle?
    a. oxygen   **b.** carbon dioxide   **c.** NADPH   **d.** chlorophyll

17. What gas is used in the first step of the Calvin cycle?
    a. oxygen   **b.** carbon dioxide   **c.** hydrogen   **d.** water

18. A carbon atom from carbon dioxide is used to change the five-carbon sugar RuBP into
    a. ATP.   **b.** two molecules.   **c.** PGA.   **d.** a six-carbon sugar.

19. How many molecules of the three-carbon sugar PGA are formed?
    a. two   **b.** one   **c.** six   **d.** three

20. ATP, NADPH, and hydrogen ions are used to convert PGA into
    a. PGAL.   **b.** glucose.   **c.** RuBP.   **d.** carbon dioxide.

21. How many rounds of the Calvin cycle are needed to form one glucose molecule?
    a. one   **b.** six   **c.** two   **d.** three

22. What two molecules leave the Calvin cycle and are combined to form glucose?
    a. RuBP   **b.** PGA   **c.** PGAL   **d.** CO_2

23. Which molecule from the Calvin cycle is used to replenish the five-carbon sugar, RuBP, which is used at the beginning of the cycle?
    a. NADP   **b.** CO_2 **c.** PGA   **d.** PGAL

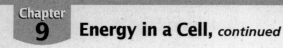

Chapter
9 **Energy in a Cell,** *continued*

Section 9.3 Getting Energy to Make ATP

In your textbook, read about the cellular respiration and fermentation.

Fill in the names of the molecules to complete the glycolysis reaction. Use these choices: 2PGAL, 4ATP, glucose, 2ADP, 2 pyruvic acid, 2NADH + 2H⁺. Then answer the questions.

Glycolysis

2ATP   **2.** _____   4ADP + 4P$_i$ **4.** _____

ENERGY

1. _____   **3.** _____   ENERGY   **5.** _____

2NAD⁺   **6.** _____

7. What happens to pyruvic acid before entering the citric acid cycle?

_____

8. What happens to the electrons carried by the NADH and FADH$_2$ molecules produced during the citric acid cycle?

_____

_____

9. During which stages of cellular respiration are ATP molecules formed?

_____

10. Why is oxygen necessary for cellular respiration?

_____

11. How is fermentation different from cellular respiration?

_____

_____

In your textbook, read about comparing photosynthesis and cellular respiration.

Answer the following question.

12. Describe two ways in which cellular respiration is the opposite of photosynthesis.

_____

_____

_____

_____

Capítulo 9 — La energía de una célula

En tu libro de texto, lee sobre la energía celular.

Completa el párrafo usando cada término una sola vez.

energía	fosfato	adenina	cargadas
ATP	enlaces químicos	funciones	ribosa

La célula requiere energía para realizar sus **(1)** _____ biológicas.

La molécula de **(2)** _____ es una fuente rápida de energía que utilizan las células.

La **(3)** _____ de esta molécula está almacenada en sus **(4)** _____ .

El ATP está compuesto por una molécula de **(5)** _____ unida al azúcar

(6) _____ . El azúcar está unido a tres moléculas

(7) _____ llamadas grupos **(8)** _____ .

En tu libro de texto, lee sobre la formación y el desdoblamiento del ATP y los usos de la energía celular.

Examina el siguiente diagrama. Después, contesta las preguntas.

Energía de los alimentos → ATP → ADP + P_i → Energía

9. ¿Cómo almacena y libera energía el ATP?

_____

_____

_____

10. ¿Para qué utilizan las células la energía liberada por el ATP?

_____

_____

_____

Capítulo **9** **La energía de una célula,** *continuación*

Sección 9.2 Fotosíntesis: La captura de energía solar

En tu libro de texto, lee acerca de cómo se captura la energía solar.

Si el enunciado es verdadero, escribe *verdadero*; **de lo contrario, modifica la sección en itálicas para hacer verdadero el enunciado.**

1. La fotosíntesis es el proceso que usan las plantas para capturar la energía solar y fabricar *glucosa.*

_____

2. Las moléculas de ATP se obtienen durante las reacciones *independientes de la luz* de la fotosíntesis.

_____

3. Se produce *dióxido de carbono* durante la fotosíntesis.

_____

4. Las reacciones dependientes de la luz de la fotosíntesis ocurren en la membrana tilacoidal de la *mitocondria.*

_____

5. La membrana tilacoidal contiene clorofila y otros pigmentos que *absorben* luz solar.

_____

En tu libro de texto, lee sobre las reacciones dependiente de la luz de la fotosíntesis.

Enumera los pasos de las reacciones dependientes de la luz, según el orden en que ocurren.

_____ **6.** La energía perdida por los electrones en su paso por la cadena de transporte electrónico se usa para obtener ATP.

_____ **7.** Los electrones pasan desde la clorofila hacia la cadena de transporte electrónico.

_____ **8.** La luz solar choca con las moléculas de clorofila en las membranas de los tilacoides.

_____ **9.** Las moléculas de $NADP^+$ se convierten en NADPH cuando transportan electrones hacia el estroma del cloroplasto.

_____ **10.** La energía de la luz solar es transferida a los electrones de la clorofila.

_____ **11.** Los electrones pasan a través de una segunda cadena de transporte electrónico.

Contesta las siguientes preguntas.

12. ¿Cómo se reemplazan los electrones perdidos por las moléculas de clorofila?

_____

_____

13. ¿Cómo producen oxígeno las plantas durante la fotosíntesis?

_____

_____

Capítulo 9 La energía de una célula, *continuación*

Sección 9.2 Fotosíntesis: La captura de la energía solar

En tu libro de texto, lee sobre las reacciones dependientes de la luz.

Marca la letra de la opción que completa mejor el enunciado o que contesta mejor la pregunta.

14. El ciclo de Calvin incluye
  a. las reacciones dependientes de la luz.
  c. las reacciones independientes de la luz.
  b. una cadena de transporte electrónico.
  d. la fotólisis.

15. El ciclo de Calvin ocurre en
  a. la mitocondria.
  c. el núcleo.
  b. el estroma.
  c. la membrana tilacoidal.

16. ¿Cuál producto de las reacciones dependientes de la luz se usa durante el ciclo de Calvin?
  a. oxígeno   **b.** dióxido de carbono **c.** NADPH   **d.** clorofila

17. ¿Cuál gas se usa durante el primer paso del ciclo de Calvin?
  a. oxígeno   **b.** dióxido de carbono **c.** hidrógeno   **d.** agua

18. Se usa un átomo de carbono del dióxido de carbono para convertir el azúcar de 5 carbonos, RuBP, en
  a. ATP.
  c. PGA.
  b. dos moléculas.
  d. un azúcar de seis carbonos.

19. ¿Cuántas moléculas del azúcar de tres carbonos, PGA, se obtienen?
  a. dos   **b.** una   **c.** seis   **d.** tres

20. Se usan ATP, NADPH y iones hidrógeno para convertir PGA en
  a. PGAL.   **b.** glucosa.   **c.** RuBP.   **d.** dióxido de carbono.

21. ¿Cuántos ciclos completos del ciclo de Calvin se requieren para obtener una molécula de glucosa?
  a. uno   **b.** seis   **c.** dos   **d.** tres

22. ¿Cuáles son las dos moléculas producto del ciclo de Calvin que se combinan para formar glucosa?
  a. RuBP   **b.** PGA   **c.** PGAL   **d.** CO_2

23. ¿Cuál molécula del ciclo de Calvin sirve para reemplazar el azúcar de cinco carbonos, RubP, que se usa al principio del ciclo?
  a. NADP   **b.** CO_2 **c.** PGA   **d.** PGAL

Capítulo 9 La energía de una célula, *continuación*

Sección 9.3 **La obtención de energía para elaborar ATP**

En tu libro de texto, lee sobre la respiración celular y la fermentación.

Anota el nombre de las moléculas para completar la reacción de glucólisis. Usa estas opciones: 2PGAL, 4ATP, glucosa, 2ADP, 2 ácido pirúvico y 2NADH + 2H⁺. Después, contesta las preguntas.

$$\textbf{Glucólisis}$$

2ATP   **2.** _____ $4ADP + 4P_i$ **4.** _____

ENERGÍA

1. _____   **3.** _____   ENERGÍA   **5.** _____

$2NAD^+$ **6.** _____

7. ¿Qué ocurre con el ácido pirúvico antes de que entre al ciclo del ácido cítrico?

_____

8. ¿Qué ocurre con los electrones transportados por las moléculas NADH y $FADH_2$, producidas durante el ciclo del ácido cítrico?

_____

_____

9. ¿Durante cuáles etapas de la respiración celular se obtienen moléculas de ATP?

_____

10. ¿Por qué se requiere oxígeno para la respiración celular?

_____

11. ¿En qué difiere la fermentación de la respiración celular?

_____

_____

En tu libro de texto, lee sobre la comparación entre la fotosíntesis y la respiración celular.

Responde la siguiente pregunta.

12. Describe dos aspectos en los cuales la respiración celular es el mecanismo opuesto a la fotosíntesis.

_____

_____

_____

_____

_____

Chapter 9   Energy in a Cell

Photosynthesis: Trapping the Sun's Energy

Complete the concept map describing photosynthesis. Use these words or phrases once: *chemical energy, oxygen, light-dependent reactions, chlorophyll, stroma, glucose, water, sunlight, energy, carbon dioxide, hydrogen ions, chloroplasts.*

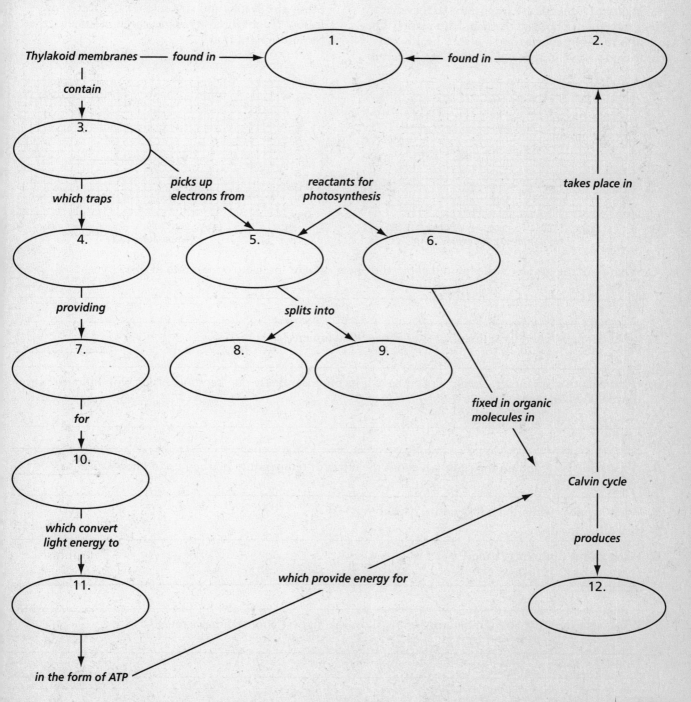

Two Factors Affecting Photosynthesis

The rate at which photosynthesis occurs is not always the same. The intensity of light, temperature, supply of carbon dioxide, supply of water, and availability of minerals are important factors that affect the rate of photosynthesis in land plants. The rate also varies by species and a plant's health and maturity. The two graphs below show the effects of light intensity and temperature on the rate of photosynthesis in land plants. These two factors affect many enzymes that control photosynthetic reactions. Study the graphs and answer the questions that follow. (Light intensity is measured in lumens, the SI unit of light flow.)

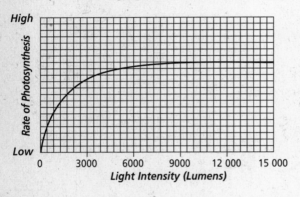

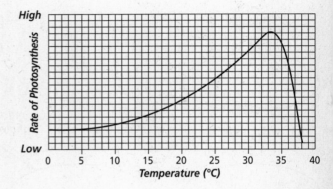

1. What does the graph on the left tell about the effect of light intensity on the rate of photosynthesis?

2. What happens when light intensity rises above 9000 lumens?

3. What adaptive advantages would a plant have if its photosynthetic rate kept increasing with light intensity above 9000 lumens?

4. What does the graph on the right tell about the effect of temperature on the rate of photosynthesis?

5. What happens when the temperature rises above 33°C?

6. What might cause this change?

7. What light intensity and temperature levels allow the highest photosynthesis rate?

Master
21   Using Energy

Section Focus

Use with Chapter 9, Section 9.1

① How is each of these organisms using energy?

② In what other ways do organisms use energy?

Master
22 Photosynthesis

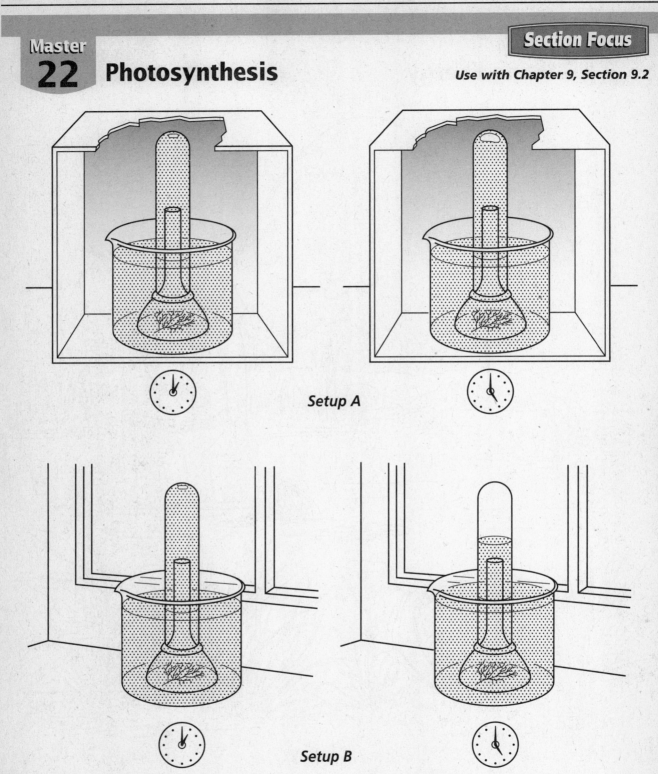

Setup A

Setup B

❶ How does the amount of gas in each test tube differ?

❷ Oxygen is a product of a process called photosynthesis, which occurs in plants. Based on the results shown, what is required for photosynthesis to occur?

Master
23 Cellular Respiration

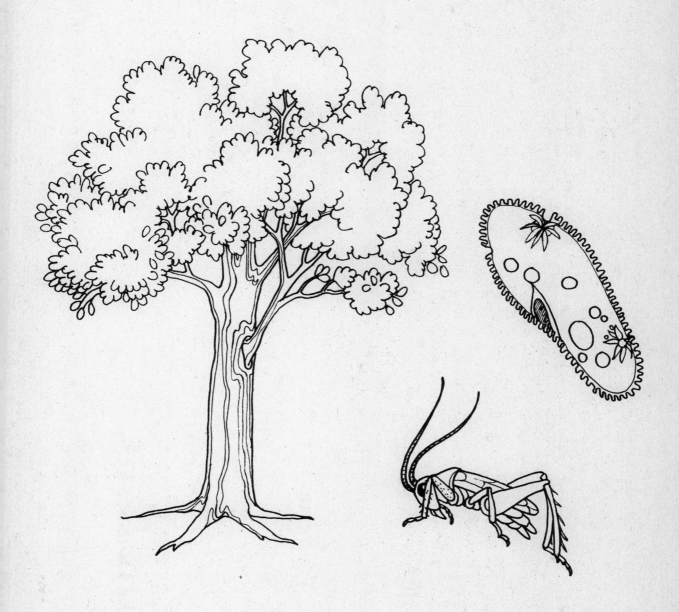

❶ Which of these organisms require energy?

❷ How does the manner in which these organisms get energy differ?

Master 11 — ATP–ADP Cycle

Use with Chapter 9, Section 9.1

Worksheet 11 ATP–ADP Cycle

1. What is the structural difference between ATP and ADP?

_____

2. Which molecules are contained in both ATP and ADP?

_____

3. In which structure, ATP or ADP, is more energy stored? Where is the energy stored?

_____

_____

4. Describe what takes place in the process of converting ADP to ATP.

_____

_____

_____

5. Describe what happens in the process of converting ATP to ADP.

_____

_____

_____

6. Explain why the reactions shown in the transparency are considered to be part of a cycle.

_____

_____

_____

_____

_____

7. Describe the role of proteins in the release of energy stored in ATP.

_____

_____

8. What are two ways that cells use energy released from the breakdown of ATP?

_____

_____

_____

Master
12   **Photosynthesis**   *Use with Chapter 9, Section 9.2*

Light-Dependent Reactions

A Light striking chloro-phyll causes elec-trons to gain energy and leave the chloro-phyll molecule. As these electrons pass down an electron transport chain, they lose energy, which is used to make ATP.

Chlorophyll molecules

C Electrons move down another electron transport chain. The electrons combine with $NADP^+$ to form NADPH.

$e^- + H^+ + NADP^+ \longrightarrow NADPH + H^+$

B Electrons from water replace electrons lost by chlorophyll. Water breaks into hydrogen and oxygen.

e^-

Energy

$ADP + P_i$

ATP

e^-

$O_2 + 4H^+$

$4e^-$

Sun

$2H_2O$

Sun

Light-Independent Reactions

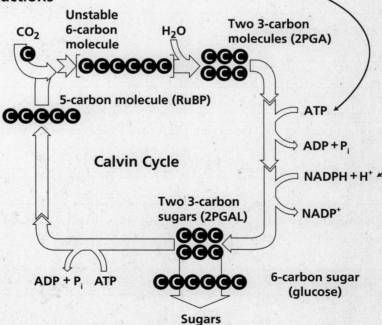

CO_2

Unstable 6-carbon molecule

H_2O

Two 3-carbon molecules (2PGA)

5-carbon molecule (RuBP)

Calvin Cycle

ATP

$ADP + P_i$

$NADPH + H^+$

$NADP^+$

Two 3-carbon sugars (2PGAL)

$ADP + P_i$ ATP

6-carbon sugar (glucose)

Sugars
Starch
Cellulose

Worksheet 12 **Photosynthesis**

1. Describe what happens when sunlight strikes chlorophyll.

_____

_____

_____

2. What happens as an electron moves down an electron transport chain?

_____

_____

_____

3. What is produced from the splitting of water during the light-dependent reactions? What is this process called?

_____

4. What is the importance of the oxygen produced during the light-dependent reactions?

_____

5. What products of the light-dependent reactions are used in the light-independent reactions?

_____

6. When does carbon fixation occur?

_____

_____

7. What is the source of energy for converting PGA into PGAL during the light-dependent reactions?

_____

_____

8. What is the final product of the light-dependent reactions? What kinds of substances are formed from it?

_____

_____

Master 13

Cellular Respiration

Glycosis

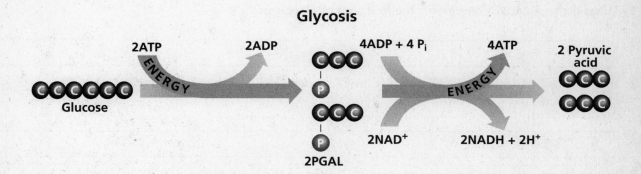

Formation of Acetyl–CoA

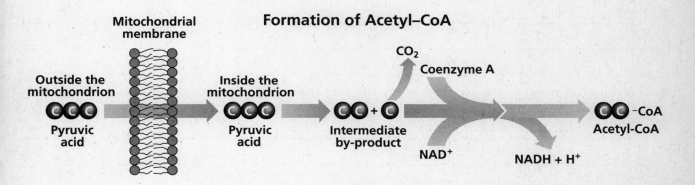

Citric Acid Cycle

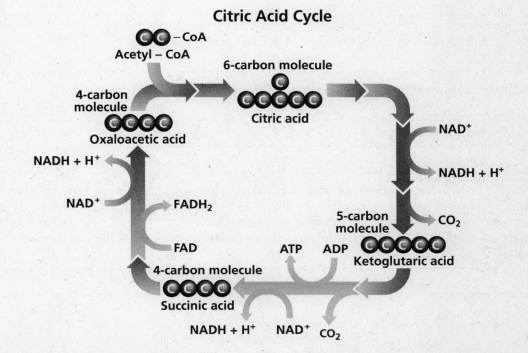

Worksheet 13 Cellular Respiration

1. What is the source of energy for the first step of glycolysis?

_____

_____

2. In glycolysis, what carbon compound is broken down? What carbon compound is the end product?

_____

_____

3. In glycolysis, what is the ratio of glucose molecules to the net number of ATP molecules at the end of the process? Explain your response.

_____

_____

_____

4. Which of the processes shown in the transparency is anaerobic? Which of the processes is aerobic?

_____

_____

5. Where does the breakdown of pyruvic acid occur?

_____

6. What is the end product of the breakdown of pyruvic acid?

_____

7. How is the breakdown of pyruvic acid related to the citric acid cycle?

_____

_____

_____

8. As citric acid breaks down, what substance is released?

_____

9. What happens to the NADH and $FADH_2$ molecules produced during cellular respiration?

_____

_____

Master
14

Electron Transport Chain

Use with Chapter 9, Section 9.3

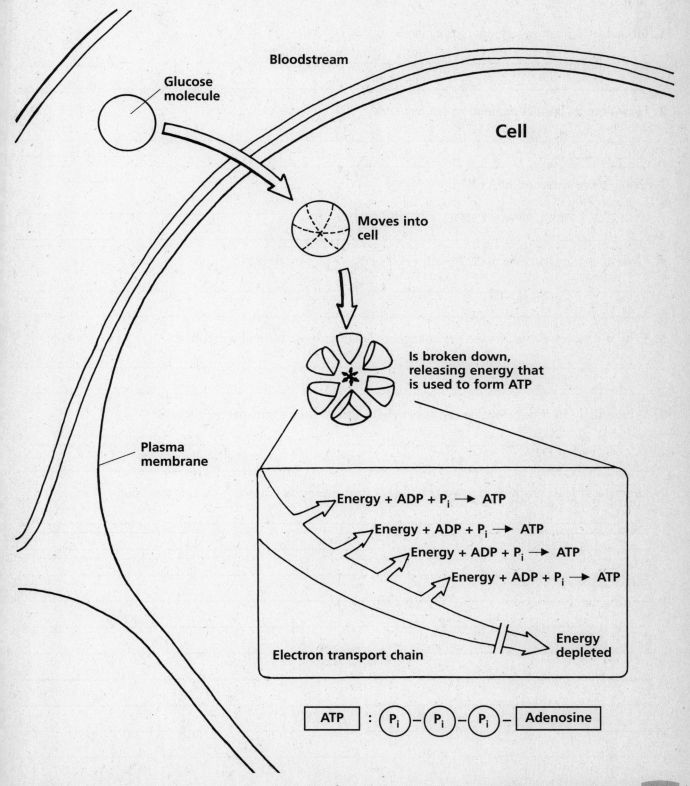

Worksheet 14 — Electron Transport Chain

1. How does a plant get glucose molecules?

_____

_____

2. How does an animal get glucose molecules?

_____

_____

3. What is the structure of ATP?

_____

_____

4. How does the structure of ATP help a cell perform its functions?

_____

_____

5. Why is it necessary to release the energy stored in glucose in small amounts?

_____

_____

6. Where in a cell is the electron transport chain shown in the transparency found?

_____

_____

7. Describe at least ten ways that your body is using energy as you work on this worksheet.

_____

_____

_____

_____

_____

_____

_____

_____

Master 15

Photosynthesis and Cellular Respiration

Use with Chapter 9, Section 9.3

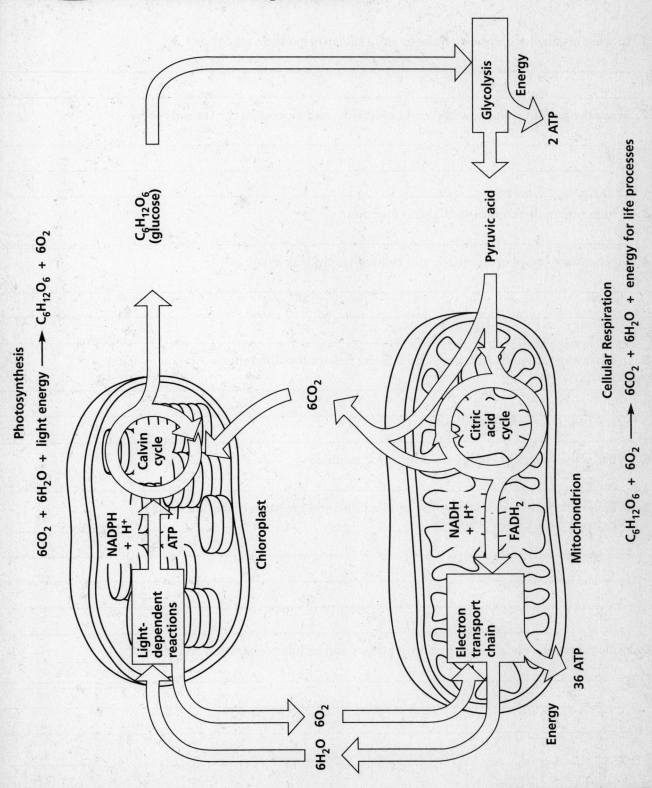

Photosynthesis

$6CO_2 + 6H_2O + \text{light energy} \longrightarrow C_6H_{12}O_6 + 6O_2$

Cellular Respiration

$C_6H_{12}O_6 + 6O_2 \longrightarrow 6CO_2 + 6H_2O + \text{energy for life processes}$

Chloroplast

Calvin cycle

Light-dependent reactions

NADPH + H$^+$

ATP

$C_6H_{12}O_6$ (glucose)

$6H_2O$ $6O_2$

$6CO_2$

Mitochondrion

Citric acid cycle

Electron transport chain

NADH + H$^+$

FADH$_2$

Glycolysis

Energy

2 ATP

Pyruvic acid

Energy

36 ATP

Worksheet 15 Photosynthesis and Cellular Respiration

1. In what organelles do photosynthesis and cellular respiration take place?

_____

_____

2. Trace the path of oxygen, water, carbon dioxide, and glucose in the transparency.

_____

_____

_____

3. Which organelle requires sunlight to function?

_____

4. In what ways are photosynthesis and cellular respiration alike?

_____

_____

_____

5. In what ways are photosynthesis and cellular respiration different?

_____

_____

_____

6. What is the source of energy used by mitochondria?

_____

7. Which two cycles are linked by the production and utilization of carbon dioxide? Where do these cycles occur?

_____

_____

_____

_____

8. Explain how the equations for photosynthesis and cellular respiration compare.

_____

_____

_____

Chapter 9 Energy in a Cell

Reviewing Vocabulary

Complete each statement.

1. The reactions in photosynthesis in which light energy from the sun is converted to chemical energy are called _____ .

2. The process by which plants trap the sun's energy to build carbohydrates is called

   _____ .

3. The transfer of electrons along a series of proteins, releasing energy as they pass, is known as an

   _____ .

4. _____ is a plant pigment that absorbs most wavelengths of light

   except green.

5. The splitting of water during photosynthesis is _____ .

6. The anaerobic process of breaking down glucose to form pyruvic acid is called

   _____ .

7. In photosynthesis, the cycle of reactions that uses carbon dioxide to synthesize glucose is known

   as the _____ .

8. A cycle of reactions in aerobic respiration that begins and ends with the same 4-carbon compound

   is the _____ .

Compare and contrast each pair of related terms.

9. aerobic process : anaerobic process

   _____

   _____

10. photosynthesis : cellular respiration

    _____

    _____

    _____

    _____

    _____

    _____

Chapter 9   Energy in a Cell, *continued*

Understanding Main Ideas (Part A)

In the space at the left, write the letter of the word or phrase that best completes the statement or answers the question.

_____ **1.** Which of the following is *not* a part of adenosine diphosphate?

    a. glucose   **b.** adenine

    c. ribose   **d.** two phosphate groups

_____ **2.** The light-independent reactions of photosynthesis take place in the

    a. thylakoids.   **b.** stroma.   **c.** mitochondria.   **d.** cytoplasm.

_____ **3.** The energy in glucose *cannot* be released by

    a. glycolysis.   **b.** the citric acid cycle.

    c. cellular respiration.   **d.** photosynthesis.

_____ **4.** Cells store energy when

    a. the third phosphate group breaks off from an ATP molecule.

    b. they break down sucrose to glucose and fructose.

    c. a third phosphate group is bonded to an ADP molecule.

    d. ions are released into the bloodstream.

_____ **5.** Leaves appear green because the green portion of the light that strikes them is

    a. changed to heat.   **b.** absorbed.   **c.** destroyed.   **d.** reflected.

_____ **6.** Which of the following equations best represents photosynthesis?

    a. $C + O_2 + H_2O \rightarrow CO_2 + HOH$ **b.** $6CO_2 + 6H_2O \rightarrow C_6H_{12}O_6 + 6O_2$

    c. $6C + 6H_2O \rightarrow C_6H_{12}O_6$ **d.** $C_6H_{12}O_6 \rightarrow 6CO_2 + 6H_2O$

_____ **7.** Kidneys use energy to move molecules and ions in order to keep the blood chemically balanced. This process is an example of cells using energy to

    a. carry on chemosynthesis.   **b.** control body temperature.

    c. transmit impulses.   **d.** maintain homeostasis.

_____ **8.** In respiration, the final electron acceptor in the electron transport chain is

    a. oxygen.   **b.** ATP.   **c.** hydrogen ions.   **d.** water.

_____ **9.** In glycolysis, ____ molecules of ATP are used in the first step and ____ molecules of ATP are produced in the second step.

    a. four, two   **b.** two, four   **c.** two, two   **d.** four, four

_____ **10.** In the process of photosynthesis, the

    a. Calvin cycle yields CO_2.   **b.** light-dependent reactions release oxygen.

    c. Calvin cycle breaks down H_2O.   **d.** light-dependent reactions produce $NADP^+$.

Chapter 9 **Energy in a Cell,** *continued*

Understanding Main Ideas (Part B)

Answer the following questions.

1. Synthesis of molecules, transmission of nerve impulses, movement of cilia, and bioluminescence are various activities of organisms.
   a. What requirement do these activities have in common?

   _____

   b. Why is ATP important in each activity?

   _____

   _____

2. Both the wine industry and the bread industry use the process of alcoholic fermentation.
   a. In what way is the use of alcoholic fermentation by these industries similar?

   _____

   _____

   b. In what way does their use of alcoholic fermentation differ?

   _____

   _____

3. In cellular respiration, the steps following glycolysis depend on whether oxygen is present. Explain.

   _____

   _____

   _____

4. Explain what is meant by carbon fixation. During which stage of photosynthesis does this process take place?

   _____

   _____

5. If you run as fast as you can, your muscles may begin to feel weak and have a burning sensation. Explain what is occurring in your muscle cells that accounts for this muscle fatigue.

   _____

   _____

   _____

   _____

Thinking Critically

Answer the following questions.

The table below shows the average yield of ATP molecules from the oxidation of glucose in eukaryotic cells.

Reaction	ATP Produced	ATP Used
Glycolysis	2	4
Citric acid cycle	2	
Electron transport chain	32	

1. What is the net production of ATP molecules by *each* of the four reactions?

   _____

   _____

2. What is the total net gain of ATP molecules per glucose molecule?

   _____

3. The combination of glycolysis and fermentation yields a net gain of 2 ATP molecules. How many molecules of ATP does fermentation yield? Explain.

   _____

   _____

   _____

In an experiment conducted to determine whether green plants take in CO_2, a biologist filled a large beaker with aquarium water to which she added bromothymol blue. She exhaled CO_2 into the solution of bromothymol blue, which made the solution turn yellow. Then she placed a sprig of *Elodea* into two test tubes. She left a third test tube without *Elodea* to serve as a control. She added the yellow bromothymol solution to all three test tubes and placed a stopper in each. Next, she placed all the test tubes in sunlight. After several hours in sunlight, the bromothymol solution in the test tubes with the *Elodea* turned blue. The bromothymol solution in the control remained yellow.

4. What conclusion can be drawn from the experiment? Explain.

   _____

   _____

   _____

Applying Scientific Methods

In 1803, Thomas Engelmann of Germany used a combination of aerobic bacteria and a filamentous alga to study the effect of various colors of the visible light spectrum on the rate of photosynthesis. He passed white light through a prism in order to separate the light into the different colors of the spectrum; then he exposed different segments of the alga to the various colors. He observed in which areas of the spectrum the greatest number of bacteria appeared. Refer to the diagram below to answer the questions that follow.

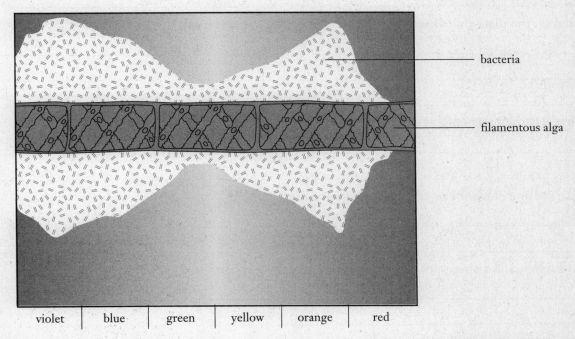

1. Using his setup, Engelmann was able to determine in which areas of the visible light spectrum the alga was releasing the most oxygen. Explain his reasoning.

   _____

   _____

2. Was determining where there was more oxygen the purpose of his experiment? If not, state the purpose.

   _____

   _____

   _____

3. How was the observation of the amount of oxygen present related to Engelmann's purpose?

   _____

   _____

   _____

Applying Scientific Methods   *continued*

4. Why did Engelmann select aerobic rather than anaerobic bacteria?

_____

_____

_____

5. Based on the diagram, what would Engelmann's conclusion be?

_____

_____

_____

6. What was the independent variable in this experiment?

_____

_____

_____

7. Describe one control Engelmann might have used. Explain.

_____

_____

_____

8. Did Engelmann's observations verify his hypothesis? Explain.

_____

_____

_____

_____

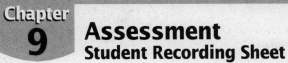

Chapter 9 Assessment
Student Recording Sheet

Chapter Assessment

Use with pages 242–243 of the Student Edition

Vocabulary Review

Write the word you chose and explain why it does not belong.

1. _____
2. _____
3. _____
4. _____
5. _____

Understanding Key Concepts

Select the best answer from the choices given and fill in the corresponding oval.

6. Ⓐ Ⓑ Ⓒ Ⓓ   10. Ⓐ Ⓑ Ⓒ Ⓓ
7. Ⓐ Ⓑ Ⓒ Ⓓ   11. Ⓐ Ⓑ Ⓒ Ⓓ
8. Ⓐ Ⓑ Ⓒ Ⓓ   12. Ⓐ Ⓑ Ⓒ Ⓓ
9. Ⓐ Ⓑ Ⓒ Ⓓ   13. Ⓐ Ⓑ Ⓒ Ⓓ

Constructed Response

Record your answers for Questions 14–16 on a separate sheet of paper.

Thinking Critically

Record your answer for Question 17 on a separate sheet of paper.

18. Fill in the correct terms to complete the concept map.

     1. _____   2. _____   3. _____   4. _____

19. **REAL WORLD BIOCHALLENGE** Follow your teacher's instructions for presenting your BioChallenge answer.

Standardized Test Practice

The Princeton Review

Part 1   Multiple Choice

Select the best answer from the choices given and fill in the corresponding oval.

20. Ⓐ Ⓑ Ⓒ Ⓓ
21. Ⓐ Ⓑ Ⓒ Ⓓ
22. Ⓐ Ⓑ Ⓒ Ⓓ
23. Ⓐ Ⓑ Ⓒ Ⓓ

Part 2
Constructed Response/Grid In

Record your answers for Questions 24 and 25 on a separate sheet of paper.

BioDigest 3 The Life of a Cell

In your textbook, read about the chemistry of life.

Label the diagram below, using these choices:

atom   electron   molecule   neutron   nucleus   proton

1. _____
2. _____
3. _____
4. _____
5. _____
6. _____

p^+

n^0

In your textbook, read about eukaryotic cells, prokaryotic cells, and organelles.

Complete each statement.

7. Every cell is surrounded by a plasma _____ .

8. _____ contain membrane-bound structures called organelles within the cell.

9. Organisms having cells without internal membrane-bound structures are called _____ .

10. The plasma membrane is composed of a _____ with embedded proteins.

11. The _____ controls cell functions.

12. Ribosomes are organelles found in the cytoplasm that produce _____ .

13. The _____ and Golgi apparatus transport and modify proteins.

14. Plant cells contain _____ that capture the sun's light energy so that it can be transformed into usable chemical energy.

15. A network of microfilaments and microtubules attached to the cell membrane give the cell _____ .

16. _____ are long projections from the surface of the plasma membrane and move in a whiplike fashion to propel a cell.

BioDigest
3 **The Life of a Cell,** *continued*

In your textbook, read about diffusion and osmosis.

Answer the following questions.

17. What is diffusion? _____

_____

18. What is osmosis? _____

_____

19. What is active transport? _____

_____

In your textbook, read about mitosis.

For each item in Column A, write the letter of the matching item in Column B.

Column A	Column B
_____ **20.** Duplicated chromosomes condense and mitotic spindles form on the two opposite ends of the cell.	**a.** anaphase
_____ **21.** Chromosomes slowly separate to opposite ends of cells.	**b.** interphase
_____ **22.** Chromosomes uncoil, spindle breaks down, and nuclear envelope forms around each set of chromosomes.	**c.** metaphase
_____ **23.** Cells experience a period of intense metabolic activity prior to mitosis.	**d.** prophase
_____ **24.** Chromosomes line up in center of cell.	**e.** telophase

In your textbook, read about energy in a cell.

Decide if each of the following statements is true. If it is not, rewrite the italicized part to make it true.

_____ **25.** Adenosine triphosphate (ATP) is the most commonly used source of *protein* in a cell.

_____ **26.** *Light-dependent* reactions convert energy into starch through the Calvin cycle.

_____ **27.** *Mitochondria* convert food energy to ATP through a series of chemical reactions.

_____ **28.** Glycolysis produces a net gain of two ATP for *every two molecules* of glucose.

BioCompendio

3 La vida de la célula

En tu libro de texto, lee sobre la química de la vida.

Rotula las partes indicadas en el siguiente diagrama. Usa las siguientes opciones:

átomo	electrón	molécula	neutrón	núcleo	protón

1. _____

2. _____

3. _____

4. _____

5. _____

6. _____

p^+

n^0

En tu libro de texto, lee sobre las células eucarióticas, las procarióticas y los organelos.

Completa cada enunciado.

7. Toda célula está rodeada por una _____ .

8. Los _____ contienen estructuras membranosas internas llamadas organelos en las células.

9. Los organismos formados por células sin estructuras membranosas internas se conocen como _____ .

10. La membrana plasmática está formada por un(a) _____ con proteínas incrustadas.

11. El(La) _____ controla las funciones de la célula.

12. Los ribosomas son organelos del citoplasma que producen _____ .

13. El(La) _____ y el aparato de Golgi transportan y modifican proteínas.

14. Las células vegetales contienen _____ , organelos que les permiten capturar la energía de la luz solar y transformarla en energía química útil para la célula.

15. Una red de microfilamentos y microtúbulos unidos a la membrana celular proporcionan _____ a la célula.

16. Los _____ son largas proyecciones que surgen de la superficie de la membrana plasmática y que se agitan como un látigo para desplazar a la célula.

BioCompendio 3

La vida de la célula,
continuación

En tu libro de texto, lee sobre la difusión y la osmosis.

Contesta las siguientes preguntas.

17. ¿Qué es la difusión? _____

_____

18. ¿Qué es la osmosis? _____

_____

19. ¿Qué es el transporte activo? _____

_____

En tu libro de texto, lee sobre la mitosis.

Anota la letra de la columna B correspondiente a cada enunciado de la columna A.

Columna A	Columna B
_____ **20.** Los cromosomas duplicados se condensan y se forma el huso mitótico en lados opuestos de la célula.	**a.** anafase
_____ **21.** Los cromosomas se separan lentamente y se desplazan hacia lados opuestos de la célula.	**b.** interfase
_____ **22.** Los cromosomas se desenrollan, se deshace el huso y se forma una cubierta nuclear alrededor de cada juego de cromosomas.	**c.** metafase
_____ **23.** La célula experimenta un período de intensa actividad metabólica antes de que ocurra la mitosis.	**d.** profase
_____ **24.** Los cromosomas se alinean en el centro de la célula.	**e.** telofase

En tu libro de texto, lee sobre la energía en la célula.

Si el enunciado es verdadero, escribe *verdadero*; de lo contrario, modifica la sección en itálicas para hacer verdadero el enunciado.

_____ **25.** La adenosina trifosfato (ATP) es la fuente de *proteínas* más común de las células.

_____ **26.** Las reacciones de la fase *dependiente de la luz* convierten energía en almidones, mediante el ciclo de Calvin.

_____ **27.** La *mitocondria* convierte la energía de los alimentos en ATP a través de una serie de reacciones.

_____ **28.** La glucólisis produce una ganancia neta de 2 ATP por *cada dos moléculas* de glucosa.

<table>
<tr><td>Unit
3</td><td>Assessment
Student Recording Sheet</td></tr>
</table>

Standardized Test Practice

Use with pages 248–249 of the Student Edition

Standardized Test Practice

Part 1   Multiple Choice

Select the best answer from the choices given and fill in the corresponding oval.

1. Ⓐ Ⓑ Ⓒ Ⓓ   10. Ⓐ Ⓑ Ⓒ Ⓓ
2. Ⓐ Ⓑ Ⓒ Ⓓ   11. Ⓐ Ⓑ Ⓒ Ⓓ
3. Ⓐ Ⓑ Ⓒ Ⓓ   12. Ⓐ Ⓑ Ⓒ Ⓓ
4. Ⓐ Ⓑ Ⓒ Ⓓ   13. Ⓐ Ⓑ Ⓒ Ⓓ
5. Ⓐ Ⓑ Ⓒ Ⓓ   14. Ⓐ Ⓑ Ⓒ Ⓓ
6. Ⓐ Ⓑ Ⓒ Ⓓ   15. Ⓐ Ⓑ Ⓒ Ⓓ
7. Ⓐ Ⓑ Ⓒ Ⓓ   16. Ⓐ Ⓑ Ⓒ Ⓓ
8. Ⓐ Ⓑ Ⓒ Ⓓ   17. Ⓐ Ⓑ Ⓒ Ⓓ
9. Ⓐ Ⓑ Ⓒ Ⓓ

Part 2   Constructed Response/Grid In

Record your answers for Questions 18–21 on a separate sheet of paper.

Contents

Teacher Support and Planning

Chapter 6 — The Chemistry of Life

Defining Vocabulary Words

Have each student make a Foldable, using the vocabulary book shown below, to define the vocabulary words for each section of the chapter.

How to Use the Foldable

Have students . . .

1. construct a vocabulary book. *If students need additional instructions to construct a vocabulary book, the bottom of this page can be reproduced and distributed to students.*

2. label each tab with a vocabulary word from the chapter.

3. under each tab, write the definition for each vocabulary word.

4. trade their Foldables with a friend and quiz each other on the contents.

Going Further

- Make an analogy or provide an example of each word.

- Make a small diagram or drawing on the front tab beside each word.

✄ -

Vocabulary Book

STEP 1 **Fold** a vertical sheet of notebook paper from side to side.

STEP 2 **Cut** along every third line of only the top layer to form tabs.

STEP 3 **Label** each tab.

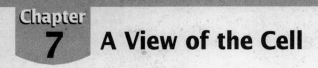

Comparing Cells

Have each student make a Foldable, using the three-tab book shown below, to compare the characteristics of plant and animal cells.

How to Use the Foldable

Have students . . .

1. construct a three-tab book. *If students need additional instructions to construct a three-tab book, the bottom of this page can be reproduced and distributed to students.*

2. label the tabs *Plant Cells*, *Both*, and *Animal Cells*.

3. list the characteristics unique to plant cells, characteristics unique to animal cells, and those characteristics common to both types of cells under the appropriate tabs.

4. use their Foldables to review plant and animal cells before the test.

Going Further

• Describe the functions of each cell characteristic and infer why those would be necessary in a plant or animal cell on the back of the Foldable.

• Draw and label detailed plant and animal cells on the appropriate tabs.

✂ --

Three-Tab Book

STEP 1 **Fold** one sheet of paper lengthwise.

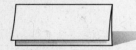

STEP 2 **Fold** into thirds.

STEP 3 **Unfold** and **draw** overlapping ovals. **Cut** the top sheet along the folds.

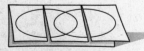

STEP 4 **Label** the ovals as shown.

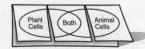

Chapter 8

Cellular Transport and the Cell Cycle

Use with Section 8.2

Illustrating the Cell Cycle

Have each student make a Foldable, using the accordion book shown below, to illustrate the steps of the cell cycle.

How to Use the Foldable

Have students . . .

1. construct an accordion book. *If students need additional instructions to construct an accordion book, the bottom of this page can be reproduced and distributed to students.*

2. label every other page *Interphase, Prophase, Metaphase, Anaphase, Telophase,* and *Cytokinesis.*

3. describe and illustrate the steps of the cell cycle.

4. use their Foldables to review what they have learned about the cell cycle.

Going Further

Critical Thinking

- Infer what the cell might look like between the stages and make illustrations that show this on the blank pages.

- Incorporate an illustrated time scale on each of the steps.

Accordion Book

STEP 1 **Fold** three vertical sheets of paper in half from top to bottom.

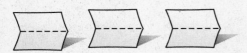

STEP 2 **Turn** the papers horizontally and **cut** the papers in half along the folds.

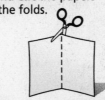

STEP 3 **Fold** the six vertical pieces in half from top to bottom.

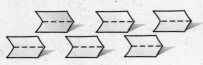

STEP 4 **Turn** the papers horizontally. **Tape** the short ends of the pieces together (overlapping the edges slightly) to make an accordion book.

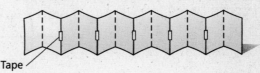

Tape

STEP 5 **Label** each fold.

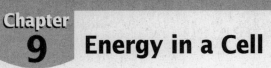

Comparing Energy Reactions

Have each student make a Foldable, using the three-tab book shown below, to help them organize events in glycolysis, the citric acid cycle, and the electron transport chain.

How to Use the Foldable

Have students . . .

1. construct a three-tab book. *If students need additional instructions to construct a three-tab book, the bottom of this page can be reproduced and distributed to students.*

2. label the top tab *Energy Reactions* and the three flaps *Glycolysis, Citric Acid Cycle,* and *Electron Transport Chain.*

3. write a list of the steps in each one of these reactions beneath the appropriate flap.

4. trade their Foldables with a friend and quiz each other on the contents.

Going Further

• Analyze each event and identify the reactants and products. Describe the importance of each product.

• Make diagrams on the front of each flap that illustrate each reaction.

✂ --

Three-Tab Book

STEP 1 **Fold** a sheet of paper in half lengthwise. Make the back edge about 5 cm longer than the front edge.

STEP 2 **Turn** the paper so the fold is on the bottom. Then **fold** it into thirds.

STEP 3 **Unfold** and **cut** only the top layer along both folds to make three tabs.

STEP 4 **Label** each tab and the top as shown.

Energy Reactions

| Glycolysis | Citric Acid Cycle | Electron Transport Chain |

Chapter 6

MiniLab 6.1
Page 3 • Determine pH

Expected Results
The approximate pH of the solutions are: lemon juice, pH 3; household ammonia, pH 11; liquid detergent, pH 10; shampoo, pH 7; and vinegar, pH 3.

Analysis
1. lemon juice and vinegar
2. household ammonia and liquid detergent
3. H^+ ions and OH^- ions. Household ammonia contains the most OH^- ions; it had the highest pH.

MiniLab 6.2
Page 4 • Investigate the Rate of Diffusion

Expected Results
The color will diffuse only a few millimeters into the cube, the exact distance depending upon the amount of time it is in the solution.

Analysis
1. Answers will depend on the amount of time the cube is in the solution.
2. The rate will be in the tenths to hundredths of millimeters per minute.

Design Your Own BioLab
Page 5 • Does temperature affect an enzyme reaction?

Data and Observations: Cooling will not deactivate the enzymes but can slow the overall reaction. Potato slices heated over 70° will not generate oxygen bubbles.

Analyze and Conclude
1. Students should describe the number of bubbles produced and their approximate duration.
2. Students should explain whether their data support or reject their hypotheses.
3. Between 20°C–50°C
4. Human tissue contains peroxidase, so the hydrogen peroxide is broken down and releases oxygen.
5. **Error Analysis** Factors to control may include the amount of time that each potato was exposed to the temperature, the sizes of the potato slices, and the amount of peroxide added. Answers for errors in results may include incomplete heating of the potato before testing.

Real World BioApplications
Page 7 • How Lean Is Lean Ground Beef?

Planning the Activity
Use this activity after students have been introduced to the various types of organic molecules in Chapter 6 of the text. Alternatively, this activity may be used as students investigate nutrition and digestion later in the course (Chapter 35).

Purpose
Students compare the cost-effectiveness of ground beef types by determining the fat content of three different samples of ground beef.

Career Applications
While most consumers are interested in the cost-effectiveness of their foods, food scientists and food technologists work to meet consumer demand for food products that are healthful, safe, palatable, and convenient. Some food technologists do research to seek new food sources; analyze food content to determine levels of vitamins, fat, sugar, or protein; and search for substitutes for harmful or undesirable additives.

Materials Tips
Materials   small samples of three types of ground beef (75% lean, 85% lean, 95% lean), balance, 250-mL beaker, hot plate, tongs, graduated cylinder, water

You may wish to review the procedure with students before they begin the activity. Instruct students to pour fat into the graduated cylinder slowly. If too much fat is spilled or left in the beaker, it will affect results.

Safety Tips
Remind students to use care when working with hot plates and when handling hot objects. Students should wear goggles and gloves throughout the activity. Instruct students to discard ground beef and fat into appropriate receptacles when the activity has been completed.

Teaching Strategies
• After students have read the opening paragraph, discuss it with them. Review the common dietary sources of fats, and the importance of fat in human physiology. Remind students about the health dangers associated with eating too much fat, and then lead into a discussion about planning healthful diets.

• Ask students to describe what happens to the size of a hamburger patty as it cooks. Elicit that the patty shrinks because water and fat are removed during the heating process. Have students discuss how the fat content of a rare and well-done hamburger might compare.

Teacher Guide & Answers

Answers to Student Worksheet

Analyze and Conclude

1. Answers will vary, but the sample of leanest ground beef should have the lowest percentage of fat, and the fattest sample will have the highest percentage of fat.

2. Answers will vary, but most students will find close, but not exact, agreement between the experimental values and those stated on the labels of the ground beef samples. Large differences may be due to inaccurate labeling on the packages, difficulty in recovering all of the fat from the samples, or inaccurate calculations.

3. Accept all reasonable answers. Many students will argue that the leanest meat is worth the added cost because too much fat is unhealthy or because more meat will remain after cooking.

Reinforcement and Study Guide
Page 9 • Section 6.1

1. cannot be
2. true
3. true
4. symbol
5. very small
6. true
7. proton
8. neutron
9. energy level
10. nucleus
11. electron
12. two in the first, eight in the second, 18 in the third
13. Isotopes are atoms of the same element that have different numbers of neutrons. Boron-11 has the same number of protons as boron-10, that is, five. Since the isotope number refers to the total number of protons and neutrons, boron-11 has six neutrons.
14. compound
15. compound
16. element
17. ionic
18. ionic
19. covalent
20. covalent

$$C_6H_{12}O_6 + 6O_2 \longrightarrow 6CO_2 + 6H_2O$$

21. Chemical equations must balance because atoms are neither created nor destroyed during a chemical reaction.

22. the subscript number to the right of each element
23. A mixture is not a solution when the substances that make up the mixture are not distributed evenly.
24. An acid forms hydrogen ions in water. A base forms hydroxide ions in water.

Page 11 • Section 6.2

1. false	8. d
2. false	9. b
3. true	10. c
4. false	11. b
5. true	12. a
6. c	13. b
7. a	

Page 12 • Section 6.3

1. true	12. glycogen
2. false	13. nucleic acids
3. false	14. lipids
4. true	15. nucleic acids
5. $C_6H_{12}O_6$	16. proteins
6. glucose	17. nucleic acids
7. fructose	18. lipids
8. $C_{12}H_{22}O_{11}$	19. proteins
9. sucrose	20. lipids
10. starch	21. proteins
11. cellulose	

Refuerzo y Guía de estudio
Página 13 • Sección 6.1

1. no puede
2. verdadero
3. verdadero
4. un símbolo
5. pequeñas
6. verdadero
7. protón
8. neutrón
9. electrón
10. núcleo
11. nivel de energía
12. dos en el primero, ocho en el segundo y 18 en el tercero
13. Los isótopos son formas de un mismo elemento que difieren en el número de neutrones. El boro-11

tiene el mismo número de protones que el boro-10, es decir, cinco. Dado que el número del isótopo se refiere a la suma de protones y neutrones, el boro-11 tiene seis neutrones.

14. compuesto
15. compuesto
16. elemento
17. enlace iónico
18. enlace iónico; enlace covalente
19. enlace covalente
20. enlace covalente
21. Las ecuaciones químicas deben estar balanceadas porque durante una reacción química no se crean ni se destruyen átomos.
22. el subíndice a la derecha de cada elemento
23. Una mezcla no es una solución cuando las sustancias que forman la mezcla no están distribuidas de manera homogénea.
24. Un ácido forma iones hidrógeno en agua. Una base forma iones hidróxilo en agua.

Página 15 • Sección 6.2

1. falso
2. falso
3. verdadero
4. falso
5. verdadero
6. c
7. a
8. d
9. b
10. c
11. b
12. a
13. b

Página 16 • Sección 6.3

1. verdadero
2. falso
3. falso
4. verdadero
5. $C_6H_{12}O_6$
6. glucosa
7. fructosa
8. $C_{12}H_{22}O_{11}$
9. sacarosa
10. almidón
11. celulosa
12. glucógeno
13. ácidos nucleicos
14. lípidos
15. ácidos nucleicos
16. proteínas
17. ácidos nucleicos
18. lípidos
19. proteínas
20. lípidos
21. proteínas

Concept Mapping
Page 17 • Properties of Water Important to Living Systems

1. attract
2. hydrogen bond with

3. other water molecules
4. resistance
5. temperature
6. cellular functions
7. capillary action
8. thin plant tubes
9. expansion
10. freezes
11. be less dense
12. break rocks
13. float in water

Critical Thinking
Page 18 • Sugars and Isomers

1. A
2. 2, 3, 4; 2, 3, 4, 5; 2, 3, 4, 5; 2, 3, 4
3. L-sugar
4. a. cis
   b. trans
   c. trans
5.

Section Focus Transparency 12
Page 19 • Elements

Purpose
- To illustrate that six elements make up more than 98% of the mass of a human

Teaching Suggestions
- Project the transparency, and explain that the substances shown in the graph are elements, the building blocks of all matter that students will learn about in this section. Explain that although there are more than 100 elements, the six elements shown in the graph make up more than 98% of the body weight of a human.
- Tell students that some of the elements that belong to the "Other Elements" category include potassium, sodium, magnesium, iron, and iodine. Explain

that although the body needs only very small amounts of these elements, they are nevertheless important. Point out that the amounts of these elements in many packaged foods can be found on the nutritional labels.

- *Answers to questions on the transparency include:*

1. The most common elements are oxygen, carbon, hydrogen, and nitrogen.
2. Students might suggest the following: oxygen—is in the air we breathe, is produced by plants, is needed by humans and other organisms to stay alive; carbon—makes up diamonds and pencil lead, is the material left after wood or paper is burned; hydrogen—is a flammable gas, the most common element in the universe (73–90%); nitrogen—is a gas in the air, is a component of laughing gas (nitrous oxide) used by dentists.

Section Focus Transparency 13
Page 20 • *Water*

Purpose

- To illustrate the importance of water and describe its characteristics

Teaching Suggestions

- Project the transparency, and point out that water can be a solid, liquid, or gas. Ask students how many times they have used water today. Have students classify their uses of water as essential or nonessential. Students will probably find that most of their uses of water are essential.

- Tell students that all organisms need water in order to survive. In fact, most organisms are made up of 70% to 95% water.

- *Answers to questions on the transparency include:*

1. Water is colorless, odorless, and tasteless and can be a liquid, solid, or gas. As a liquid, water flows easily and dissolves many substances. As a solid, water is less dense and expands as it freezes. As a gas, water becomes water vapor and causes humidity.
2. Organisms need water for life processes to occur. For example, water is needed to digest food, to transport food and other materials to cells, to remove wastes from cells, and to produce body parts.

Section Focus Transparency 14
Page 21 • *Elements in Different Combinations*

Purpose

- To illustrate that many different compounds can be made with different combinations of only a few elements

Teaching Suggestions

- Before projecting the transparency, ask students how many letters there are in our alphabet. (26) Then ask how many words they think are in a standard English dictionary. (more than 150,000)

- Project the transparency, and have students study the words. Then ask what the words have in common. (The words are composed of the same four letters—*a*, *e*, *r*, and *t*.) Discuss how the 26 letters of the alphabet are combined in different ways to make all the words in the English language.

- *Answers to questions on the transparency include:*

1. Four different letters make up the words. Other possible words are ate, art, and rare.
2. The natural elements can be combined in different amounts and in different arrangements, just as the four letters are combined in different amounts and arrangements to make different words.

Basic Concepts Transparency 4
Page 23 • *Atomic Structure*

Purpose

- To show the basic structure of an atom

Teaching Suggestions

- Project the base transparency and challenge students to identify the structures shown. Then superimpose the overlay to reinforce or correct student responses.

- Emphasize that the atoms shown in the transparency are the smallest particles of oxygen and hydrogen that still retain all the characteristics of these elements.

- Point out that neutrons contribute to the mass of an atom. Atoms with the same number of protons but different numbers of neutrons have a different mass but represent the same element. Such atoms are called isotopes.

Extension: Models

- Organize students into cooperative work groups and have them use spheres of various sizes such as balls, marbles, and beads; glue; wires; or other materials to construct models of various atoms. Assign a different atom to each group. Include two or more isotopes of the same element.

Answers to Student Worksheet

1. neutrons and protons
2. The nucleus is positively charged.
3. Electrons exist around the nucleus in regions called energy levels.
4. Each energy level can hold a certain maximum number of electrons. The first energy level can hold a maximum of two electrons, the second level can hold a maximum of eight electrons, and the third level can hold up to 18 electrons.
5. Because atoms have no net charge, the number of negatively charged electrons must equal the number of positively charged protons.
6. Two electrons are in the first energy level, and six electrons are in the second energy level.
7. A hydrogen atom has only one proton, one electron, and no neutrons.
8. The characteristics of hydrogen and oxygen are determined by the number and location of their protons and electrons.

Basic Concepts Transparency 5
Page 25 • Covalent and Ionic Bonding

Purpose

- To compare and contrast covalent and ionic bonding

Teaching Suggestions

- Emphasize that the number of electrons in the outer energy level of an atom determines how the atom will behave in a chemical reaction, that is, whether the atom will share, gain, or lose electrons.

- Project part 5a of the transparency and ask students how the atoms in a water molecule are held together (by covalent bonds). Provide examples of how atoms differ in their capacity to form covalent bonds. Hydrogen, for example, can form only one covalent bond, but carbon can form four covalent bonds.

- Project part 5b of the transparency and ask students to compare the sodium and chlorine atoms before and after they have reacted to form sodium chloride. Point out that the transfer of the electron from sodium to chlorine did not change the identity of the atoms, only their charge.

Extension: Research

- Have students look up the structures of various amino acids, which are the building blocks of proteins. The atoms of amino acids are joined by covalent bonds. Students should determine the electron configuration of the atoms in an amino acid, which are C, H, O, N, and usually S, and identify the number of bonds that link each atom to the next.

Answers to Student Worksheet

1. Water is a liquid at room temperature, whereas the elements that comprise it—oxygen and hydrogen—are gases.
2. Hydrogen requires two electrons in the outer energy level in order to be stable, whereas oxygen, sodium, and chlorine each require eight electrons in the outer energy level in order to be stable.
3. Two hydrogen atoms share an electron with one oxygen atom, forming water. The shared electrons form covalent bonds between the atoms.
4. A molecule of water has no overall charge.
5. A sodium atom loses one electron from its third energy level and becomes a positive ion. This electron is gained by the chlorine atom, which becomes a negative ion. The ions are held together by the attraction of their opposite charges, forming sodium chloride. The attractive force between the atoms is an ionic bond.
6. A two-atom hydrogen molecule is more chemically stable than individual atoms of hydrogen because each hydrogen atom within the molecule has a full outer energy level, due to the sharing of electrons.
7. The transmission of nerve impulses and muscle contraction are examples of biological processes that require ions.

Reteaching Skills Transparency 8
Page 29 • Life Molecules

Purpose

- To compare and contrast the structures and functions of the basic organic molecules
- Skill: Interpreting scientific illustrations

Teaching Suggestions

- Present the transparency and discuss the idea that although all biological molecules contain the same kinds of atoms, such as carbon, hydrogen, oxygen, and nitrogen, the way those atoms are arranged affects their role in living systems.

Teacher Guide & Answers

- Review the symbols of elements used in each molecule. Note that *R* in a protein indicates that a group of atoms will attach at that place in the molecule. The type of protein is determined by the identity of the atoms in the *R* group.

- Have students compare the five types of organic molecules. They should note the shape of the molecules as well as the types of atoms that make up the molecules.

Extension: Model

- Have models of the five types of organic molecules available in class so that students can observe them as three-dimensional entities.

Answers to Student Worksheet

1. Carbon atoms have four electrons available for bonding in the outer energy level. To become stable, carbon atoms form four covalent bonds. These bonds can be single, double, or triple bonds. As a result, carbon atoms can form a wide variety of molecules.

2. A carbohydrate is an organic compound composed of carbon, hydrogen, and oxygen, with a ratio of about two hydrogen atoms and one oxygen atom for every carbon atom.

3. A monosaccharide is a simple sugar. A disaccharide consists of two monosaccharides linked together. A polysaccharide is a polymer composed of many monosaccharide subunits.

4. a. used as food storage in plants

   b. used as food storage in mammals

   c. used to form cell walls of plants and to give plants structural support

5. Lipids, commonly called fats and oils, are organic compounds that have a large proportion of C–H bonds and less oxygen than carbohydrates. Lipids are used for long-term energy storage, insulation, and protective coatings.

6. a. a large, complex polymer composed of carbon, hydrogen, oxygen, nitrogen, and usually sulfur

   b. the basic building block of proteins

   c. the covalent bond formed between amino acids

7. Proteins are the building blocks of many structural components of organisms, such as hair, horns, hoofs, and nails. Proteins are also important in muscle contraction, transporting oxygen in the bloodstream, providing immunity, regulating other proteins, and carrying out chemical reactions.

8. Nucleotides are made up of carbon, hydrogen, oxygen, nitrogen, and phosphorus atoms arranged in three groups—a base, a simple sugar, and a phosphate group. Nucleotides are the subunits of nucleic acids, which are complex molecules (either RNA or DNA) that store information in the form of a code.

Chapter Assessment
Page 31 • *Reviewing Vocabulary*

1. d	8. a
2. h	9. isotopes
3. c	10. compounds
4. e	11. covalent
5. b	12. acid
6. f	13. nucleotides
7. g	14. diffusion

Page 32 • *Understanding Main Ideas (Part A)*

1. a	7. b
2. b	8. d
3. c	9. a
4. d	10. c
5. a	11. b
6. d	12. b

Page 33 • *Understanding Main Ideas (Part B)*

1. Magnesium chloride; it is formed by ionic bonding because two electrons are transferred from the magnesium atom, one to each chlorine atom, to form two chloride ions and one magnesium ion.

2. Hydrogen fluoride; it is formed by covalent bonding because two electrons, one from each atom, are shared by the atoms that make up the hydrogen fluoride molecule.

3. two

4. magnesium

Page 34 • *Thinking Critically*

1. 8.3–10.0; colorless to red

2. an acid

3. fatty acid

4. A is saturated because it contains only single carbon–carbon bonds. B is unsaturated because it contains a double carbon–carbon bond.

5. glycerol

Page 35 • *Applying Scientific Methods*

1. Tube 1 is the control because it contains the substances, egg white and water, that are found in all four test tubes. The control is important because it acts as a standard to which the other test tubes can be compared.

2. The independent variable is the substance that may affect the digestion of proteins. The dependent variable is the digestion of the egg white.

3. Hydrochloric acid helps pepsin digest proteins in the stomach.

4. Yes; the pepsin digested the egg white more quickly in the presence of hydrochloric acid.

5. If test tubes 3 and 4 showed the same results, it could be concluded that hydrochloric acid does not help pepsin to digest proteins in the stomach.

6. The results indicated that the hydrochloric acid itself does not digest proteins in the stomach.

7. Pepsin digests proteins slightly at body temperature. In the presence of hydrochloric acid, the digestion of proteins by pepsin is much more efficient.

Student Recording Sheet
Page 37

Answers can be found on page 168 in the Teacher Wraparound Edition.

Teacher Guide & Answers

Chapter 7

MiniLab 7.1
Page 41 • Measuring Objects Under a Microscope

Procedure

1. 700 μm
2. 25 μm
3. 60–100 μm (depending on race and/or hair color)

Analysis

1. No. An object's size does not change, only its magnification changes.
2. Observations under low and high power should be close. Error in estimating may be the cause of differing measurements.

MiniLab 7.2
Page 42 • Cell Organelles

Analysis

1. cell wall, cytoplasm; cell wall, cytoplasm, nucleus
2. Staining allows certain organelles to be more easily observed.

Investigate BioLab
Page 43 • Observing and Comparing Different Cell Types

Procedure

Data Table

	Bacillus subtilis	*Elodea*	Frog Blood
Organelles observed	No visible internal organelles	Chloroplasts, vacuole, cell wall	Nucleus
Prokaryote or eukaryote	Prokaryote	Eukaryote	Eukaryote
From a multicellular or unicellular organism	Unicellular	Multicellular	Multicellular
Diagram (with size in micrometers, μm)	8 μm	30 μm	15 μm

Check students' diagrams.

Analyze and Conclude

1. *Bacillus subtilis* is prokaryotic—no internal organelles are visible. *Elodea* and blood cells are eukaryotic—internal organelles are observed.
2. *Elodea* is from a plant—cell wall and chloroplasts are visible. Blood cells are from an animal—no cell wall or chloroplasts are visible.

3. Eukaryote cells are larger—the prokaryotic cell is less than 5 μm while both eukaryotic cells are in the range of 10–100 μm.
4. Students can draw or describe the parts of the cells they observed. A review of Section 7.3 may help their descriptions of the functions of the organelles.
5. **Error Analysis** You may have used millimeters (mm) as your measurement standard instead of micrometers.

Real World BioApplications
Page 45 • Inside the Artificial Kidney Machine

Planning the Activity

This activity can be used to reinforce the general principles of diffusion discussed in Chapter 7 of the text and to illustrate the importance of homeostasis in organisms. Alternatively, this activity can be used after students have studied excretion and the function of kidneys later in the course (Chapter 37).

Purpose

Students relate their understanding of diffusion and homeostasis to the function of a nephron. They learn about the process of hemodialysis in an artificial kidney machine.

Career Applications

A renal dialysis technician generally works under the direct supervision of a registered nurse. The technician is responsible for setting up equipment, preparing dialysate solutions, performing venipuncture, and monitoring patient responses during the dialysis procedure. The technician must be attentive to detail and follow exact procedures. At the same time, he or she must be responsive to the individual patient's comfort and concerns.

Teaching Strategies

- After students read the opening section, discuss with them the importance of homeostasis in organisms. Stress that homeostasis works on all levels of organization, from the level of the cell up to the level of the whole organism.

- Briefly discuss the role of the kidney in human physiology. Explain that the kidney is considered to be a body or blood filter, and nephrons are the tiny filtering units of the kidney.

- It may be necessary to explain and discuss the illustration of the nephron in Figure 1 with students as they complete Part A. Review the principles of passive and active transport with students, then point out how nephron function involves both passive and active transport of materials. Be sure students understand the pathway of materials through the nephron.

Answers to Student Worksheet

Part A

1. urea, uric acid, glucose, and salts
2. The glomerulus and Bowman's capsule actually filter the blood.
3. These substances become more concentrated because water is reabsorbed into the capillaries.
4. Glucose is reabsorbed into capillaries after passing through Bowman's capsule.

Part B

1. Waste materials in the blood diffuse through the tubing into the solution surrounding the tubing. Answers should discuss the idea of substances moving from an area of high concentration to an area of low concentration.
2. Waste materials would not diffuse because the concentrations of waste substances in the surrounding fluid would be similar to those in the blood.
3. You would expect to find blood cells, water, glucose, and proteins in the tube leading back to the person's vein.
4. These substances don't leave the tubing because either they are too big to pass through the selectively permeable tubing, as with the blood cells and large proteins, or there is no net movement out of the tubing because the concentrations of these substances in the surrounding fluid were similar to those in the blood.

Reinforcement and Study Guide

Page 47 • Section 7.1

1. f
2. b
3. e
4. a
5. d
6. c
7. prokaryotes
8. prokaryotes
9. eukaryotes
10. prokaryotes
11. eukaryotes

Page 48 • Section 7.2

1. balance
2. homeostasis
3. glucose
4. plasma membrane
5. selective permeability
6. organism
7. false
8. true
9. false
10. false
11. true
12. true
13. false

Page 49 • Section 7.3

1. vacuole
2. Golgi apparatus
3. ribosomes
4. endoplasmic reticulum
5. cytoplasm
6. nucleus
7. chloroplast
8. lysosomes
9. ribosomes
10. vacuole
11. cell wall
12. mitochondria or chloroplast
13. Golgi apparatus
14. chloroplast
15. plastids
16. true
17. cytoskeleton
18. true
19. locomotion
20. Cilia
21. less
22. unicellular
23. eukaryotic
24. animal cell
25. plant cell
26. plasma membrane
27. lysosome
28. cell wall
29. chloroplast
30. large vacuole

Teacher Guide & Answers

Refuerzo y Guía de estudio
Página 51 • Sección 7.1

1. f
2. b
3. e
4. a
5. d
6. c
7. procariotas
8. procariotas
9. eucariotas
10. procariotas
11. eucariotas

Página 52 • Sección 7.2

1. equilibrio
2. homeostasis
3. glucosa
4. membrana plasmática
5. permeabilidad selectiva
6. organismo
7. falso
8. verdadero
9. falso
10. falso
11. verdadero
12. verdadero
13. falso

Página 53 • Sección 7.3

1. vacuola
2. aparato de Golgi
3. ribosomas
4. retículo endoplásmico
5. citoplasma
6. núcleo
7. cloroplasto
8. lisosomas
9. ribosomas
10. vacuola
11. pared celular
12. mitocondria
13. aparato de Golgi
14. cloroplasto
15. plástidos
16. verdadero
17. citoesqueleto
18. verdadero
19. locomoción
20. cilios
21. menos
22. unicelulares
23. eucariotas
24. célula animal
25. célula vegetal
26. membrana plasmática
27. vacuola
28. pared celular
29. cloroplasto
30. vacuola

Concept Mapping
Page 55 • Recycling in the Cell

1. Lysosomes
2. vacuoles
3. tail
4. digestive enzymes
5. cell proteins
6. digestive enzymes
7. digesting it
8. a membrane
9. worn-out cell parts
10. food particles
11. bacteria and viruses

Critical Thinking
Page 56 • Cell Organelles and Their Functions

1. a. Mitochondria break down and release stored energy for the cell.

   b. In most people, the activity of muscles and nerve tissues decreases with age and the decrease may be because fewer mitochondria are releasing energy to sustain activity. The DNA difference may be the cause of fewer properly functioning mitochondria in older people.

2. The decrease in activity of heart muscle with age may be caused by defective DNA.

3. All three symptoms involve disorders of muscle tissues, which depend on mitochondria releasing energy to function properly.

4. Lysosomes; lysosomes contain digestive enzymes, which are used to digest worn-out cell parts and viruses among other things.

5. Constant doses of alcohol must have caused the liver to produce more smooth endoplasmic reticulum for detoxification.

Section Focus Transparency 15
Page 57 • Gathering Information with Scientific Tools

Purpose
- To illustrate that scientific tools help scientists gather more precise information

Teaching Suggestions
- Project the transparency, and have students observe the three images. Explain that the images are of a unicellular organism called a paramecium and that each image was produced by a different kind of microscope. (Figure A—light microscope; Figure B—TEM; Figure C—SEM)
- Explain that two of the microscopes, the TEM and the SEM, use beams of electrons to produce images. Have students recall what they learned about electrons in Chapter 6.
- *Answers to questions on the transparency include:*

1. The image produced by the light microscope shows the entire organism, but does not show much detail. The image produced by the TEM shows greater magnification and therefore greater detail. The SEM shows the paramecium in a three-dimensional image, but only the surface is visible.
2. Answers might include: The light microscope could be used to view entire organisms that are too large to be seen by the TEM. The TEM would be a good choice to view the details of cell parts. The SEM shows the surface of the specimen in a three-dimensional image.

Section Focus Transparency 16
Page 58 • Movement of Materials

Purpose
- To illustrate that membranes can be selective

Teaching Suggestions
- Project the transparency, and have students describe what is happening. Be sure that students recognize that the starch particles are not present on both sides of the membrane.
- Review with students what they learned about the plasma membrane in the previous section. Have students recall that the plasma membrane is selectively permeable, like the membrane in the illustration. Point out that in this section, students will learn more about the plasma membrane and how it controls movement of materials into and out of the cell.

- *Answers to questions on the transparency include:*
1. The sugar is passing through the membrane; the starch is not.
2. The membrane controls what materials move through it.

Section Focus Transparency 17
Page 59 • Plant and Animal Cells

Purpose
- To introduce the similarities and differences between plant and animal cells

Teaching Suggestions
- Project the transparency, and begin a discussion of the differences between plants and animals—how they obtain food, their internal support structures, and others. List these on the board.
- Ask students to think about how these differences might make the cells of animals and plants different.
- Add to your list some similarities between plants and animals and how these might be found on a cellular level.
- Keep the lists on the board as you discuss the parts of the cell in Section 7.3. Students can help connect the cell parts to the functions they listed.
- *Answers to questions on the transparency include:*

1. Plants and animals need food and water to stay alive. Students may also note that plants need sunlight. Animals (especially humans) need some sunlight as well.
2. Depending on their knowledge of cells, students' responses could include: Plant and animals cells will each have a nucleus, plasma membrane, ribosomes, cytoskeleton, Golgi apparatus, endoplasmic reticulum, lysosomes, mitochondria, and vacuoles. In addition, plants contain chloroplasts to make food in photosynthesis and have a cell wall for support.

Basic Concepts Transparency 6
Page 61 • Plasma Membrane

Purpose
- To show the bilayer structure of the plasma membrane

Teaching Suggestions
- Demonstrate the formation of a thin lipid layer by placing a drop of baby oil on the surface of a beaker of water.

Teacher Guide & Answers

- Discuss the fluid mosaic model as an operational definition of the plasma membrane.

- Point out that the degree of fluidity of the plasma membrane is related to the proportion of saturated and unsaturated fatty acids it contains. The higher the proportion of saturated fatty acids, the less fluid the membrane will be. Relate the property of fluidity to the freezing temperatures of saturated and unsaturated fatty acids.

- The filaments of cytoskeleton illustrated with the plasma membrane provide support for the membrane. The cytoskeleton is more fully discussed in Section 7.3.

Extension: Laboratory

- Make a culture of *Paramecium*. Place some yeast that have been colored with Congo red in the culture for half an hour. Have students observe the membranes that form around the colored yeast particles inside the paramecia.

Answers to Student Worksheet

1. The phospholipid in the transparency is a molecule consisting of a phosphate group and two fatty acid chains linked to glycerol.
2. The phosphate, or polar end, is attracted to water.
3. There are two layers of phospholipids in the plasma membrane, arranged with the phosphate ends facing the outside of each layer and the fatty acid ends facing the inside.
4. Many proteins regulate the permeability of the membrane to various substances, some function as enzymes, and others serve as markers that enable the immune system to distinguish an organism's own cells from foreign cells.
5. The model shows phospholipid molecules that are not chemically bonded to one another but, rather, are free to move sideways through their layer, allowing the membrane to behave like a fluid.
6. It would be very fluid.
7. The cholesterol molecules help stabilize the phospholipids.

Basic Concepts Transparency 7
Page 63 • *The Cell*

Purpose
- To review the structure and function of cell organelles

Teaching Suggestions
- Project the base transparency and ask students if they can identify the organelles in the plant and animal cells. Then use the overlay to reinforce or correct student responses.

- Many students think of cells as two-dimensional objects. Impress upon them that all cells and cell organelles are three-dimensional.

- Students often consider all cells to be spheres or cubes. Point out that cells come in many different shapes and sizes. Also explain that every cell does not contain every organelle. For example, human red blood cells do not have a nucleus when they are mature.

Extension: Enrichment Activity

- Have students describe common objects that have functions similar to the organelles. Examples: the nucleus may be thought of as a computer that stores and uses information; the cell wall may be thought of as the protective covering placed on an automobile that keeps out sunlight and dust.

Answers to Student Worksheet

1. Endoplasmic reticulum, Golgi apparatus, ribosome, vacuole, cytoskeleton, lysosome, plasma membrane, mitochondria, nucleus, and nucleolus
2. lysosome
3. chloroplast
4. The central vacuole is a storage organelle.
5. A cell containing many chloroplasts would carry on a lot of photosynthesis to make food for the plant.
6. Some plant cells do not photosynthesize. Examples of cells that do not engage in photosynthesis are the interior cells of stems and most root cells.
7. ribosomes
8. Mitochondria release energy necessary for movement.

Reteaching Skills Transparency 9
Page 65 • *The Optical Microscope*

Purpose
- To review the parts of a light microscope and their functions

- Skill: Interpreting scientific illustrations

Teaching Suggestions
- Project the transparency and have students address the questions in the worksheet

- Point out that the coarse adjustment should never be used to focus the high-power objective. Moreover, focusing should begin by lowering the objective to a point near the slide while viewing the objective lens from the side so that it does not contact the slide.

Then, while looking through the eyepiece, students should use the adjustment knobs to draw the objective up until the specimen is in focus.

- Warn students that, when using a microscope with a mirror, they should never use sunlight as a light source because reflected sunlight may damage the eyes.

Extension: Research Activity

- Have students prepare slides of a variety of specimens and observe them under low and high power of a light microscope. Students should make drawings of what they see and include these in their reports. Students should make sure that specimens are thin enough to permit light to pass through.

Answers to Student Worksheet

1. The diaphragm is used to regulate the amount of light that passes through the specimen.
2. To change the objective lens, you must rotate the revolving nosepiece.
3. The coarse adjustment knob is turned to focus the image under low power.
4. A light source transmits light through the diaphragm, specimen, and lenses, allowing you to view the specimen.
5. The term *compound* refers to the fact that modern light microscopes consist of two sets of lenses, one in the eyepiece and the other in the objective.
6. The specimen slide is positioned on the stage of the microscope and held in place by the stage clips.
7. The total magnification is 10 3 45 5 4503.
8. Van Leeuwenhoek's microscope had only a single magnifying lens, whereas compound microscopes have a series of lenses, thereby allowing for greater magnification.
9. A compound light microscope can magnify objects only to about 1500 times their actual size because of the limitations imposed by light waves. TEMs use electrons, rather than light. They can magnify objects hundreds of thousands of times and produce images that are two-dimensional. However, because the specimen must be viewed in a vacuum, only dead cells or organisms can be viewed.

Reteaching Skills Transparency 10
Page 67 • *Eukaryotic Cell Structure and Organelles*

Purpose
- To understand the basic structures contained within an animal cell
- Skill: Interpreting scientific illustrations

Teaching Suggestions
- Present the transparency. Emphasize the fact that although it discusses structures in an animal cell, all of the structures are also found in plant cells.
- Discuss the function of each of the cellular structures in the transparency.
- Elicit information about animal cell structures that are not included in the transparency, such as chromatin, cytoplasm, vacuoles, lysosomes, cilia, and flagella.
- Elicit information about structures not included here but found in plant cells and various bacteria, such as cell walls and chloroplasts.

Extension: Display
- The generalized cell presented in this chapter becomes very specialized in multicellular organisms. Prepare a display of specialized cells so students can observe that all specialized cells have all the elements discussed in this chapter in addition to the specialized structures for the cell's particular function. Include photos of such cells as nerve cells, muscle cells, and heart muscle cells.

Answers to Student Worksheet
1. manages cell functions; includes chromatin and the nucleolus, which produces ribosomes; involved in protein synthesis
2. boundary between the cell and its external environment; allows cell to vary shape as needed; controls the movement of materials that enter and exit the cell
3. provides a large surface area on which chemical reactions can take place; site for lipid synthesis; is cell's delivery system, providing materials for ribosomes as they synthesize proteins
4. breaks down food molecules to release energy, which is then stored in other molecules that can power cell reactions easily
5. receives newly synthesized proteins and lipids from the ER and distributes them to the plasma membrane and other cell organelles; chemically modifies proteins, then repackages them for distribution to final destination
6. provides support for organelles; also helps maintain cell shape; includes microtubules and microfilaments

Chapter Assessment
Page 69 • *Reviewing Vocabulary*

1. cell wall
2. nucleus
3. chromatin

4. endoplasmic reticulum
5. chlorophyll
6. cytoskeleton
7. chloroplasts
8. Transport proteins
9. cilia
10. mitochondria
11. prokaryote
12. plasma membrane
13. organelles
14. ribosomes
15. lysosomes

Page 70 • Understanding Concepts (Part A)

1. a	6. b
2. d	7. a
3. b	8. a
4. d	9. c
5. b	10. c

Page 71 • Understanding Concepts (Part B)

1. A is the ribosomes; B is the DNA; C is the plasma membrane; D is the cell wall.

2. Scientists would classify this bacterium as a prokaryote because it has no membrane-bound internal structures and it does not have a distinct nucleus, even though it does contain DNA.

3. Mitochondria are organelles that produce energy for cell reactions; active cells usually have more mitochondria than do less active cells. It would be reasonable to conclude that the number of mitochondria is in direct relation to the amount of work done by the cells.

4. Cells could not be studied in detail until the technology was available to develop efficient microscopes.

Page 72 • Thinking Critically

1. Both the glycocalyx and the cell wall surround the plasma membrane. The cell wall is made of cellulose and is fairly thick, stiff, and rigid; the glycocalyx is a complex carbohydrate that is quite thin and flexible. The glycocalyx is bonded to the plasma membrane; the cell wall is not.

2. Lysosomes also contain digestive enzymes, but the membrane surrounding a lysosome prevents these enzymes from leaving the lysosome and destroying the cell's proteins. If the lysosome membrane should break down, the contents would digest the cell's proteins just as the stomach enzymes may digest the stomach.

3. The difference between prokaryotic and eukaryotic cells is greater because these two types of cells differ in basic cell organization. Eukaryotic cells are characterized by membrane-bound organelles. Prokaryotic cells do not have membrane-bound organelles and must carry on all essential life processes without them. Plant and animal cells are both eukaryotic and have many organelles in common (for example, nucleus, mitochondria, endoplasmic reticulum, Golgi apparatus, lysosomes). Animal cells lack a cell wall and the plastids found in plant cells.

Page 73 • Applying Scientific Methods

1. that the nucleus would retain its shape even when its contents were removed

2. A fibrous protein network (nuclear matrix) was observed to be present in the nucleus.

3. to verify or disprove the presence of a nuclear matrix reported by scientist S

4. The variable was the method and substance used to remove the contents of the nucleus. Each scientist used a different substance.

5. to demonstrate that the nuclear matrix did not result from any chemical reactions but actually existed as an independent structure

6. Sample answer: A scientist could detach chromatin strands from the fibrous layer and observe whether or not chromosomes form when the cell is ready to reproduce.

7. He was trying to determine the structure of the plasma membrane.

8. no

9. Many scientists, including the Dutch, experimented to determine the actual arrangement of the lipids in the plasma membrane.

10. that the membrane consists of a double layer of lipid molecules

11. Because the surface area of the red blood cell was only half the surface area of the lipids from that cell, the cell covering must be a double layer of lipids.

12. the "fat sandwich" model

13. A new procedure, "freeze-fracture," had to be developed before scientists could observe the actual arrangement of lipids and proteins.

Student Recording Sheet
Page 75

Answers can be found on page 192 in the Teacher Wraparound Edition.

Chapter 8

MiniLab 8.1
Page 79 • Cell Membrane Simulation

Expected Results
The inside of the bag will be purple indicating passage of iodine into the bag. The outside of the bag will be rust color, indicating starch did not pass out of the bag.

Analysis
1. Start—starch was clear, iodine was rust; end—starch was purple, iodine was rust.
2. Iodine moved into the bag as shown by the purple color.
3. Students may suggest that the plastic bag is an adequate model because it allows iodine to cross; but not the starch. Others may suggest that the real membranes are more complex in their response. Both observations are correct.

MiniLab 8.2
Page 80 • Seeing Asters

Analysis
1. Asters are starlike projections of microtubules associated with centrioles. Asters are found at the cell poles in prophase.
2. Asters are not critical because plant cells undergo mitosis without the structures.
3. Sketches should show the chromatic coils forming visible chromosomes. Asters can be included for the animal cell.

Investigate BioLab
Page 81 • Where is mitosis most common?

Sample Data

Data Table

Phase	Area X	Area Y
Interphase	95	36
Prophase	15	0
Metaphase	5	0
Anaphase	2	0
Telophase	4	0

Analyze and Conclude
1. X, Y; student totals will vary to support the conclusions.
2. X; this was the area showing cells undergoing mitosis at the highest rate.

3. an area of rapid growth such as skin, hair follicles, intestine lining
4. Answers may vary—the phase has already occurred, the phase has not yet occurred, area of view is not rapidly growing, incorrect observation or recording stage.
5. **Error Analysis** Errors might result from counting cells out of the area of greatest growth, or by not counting enough cells.

Real World BioApplications
Page 83 • Osmosis and the Case of the Sad Salad

Planning the Activity
This activity should be used after students have studied the concept of diffusion in Chapter 8 of the text. It can be used to reinforce the study of osmosis and the movement of other materials across the plasma membrane of cells.

Purpose
Students investigate osmosis as they determine how carrot cells respond to two different environments.

Career Applications
Biological technicians often work with cellular biologists who study the mechanisms of cell transport in living organisms and infectious agents. These technicians usually work in laboratories and must be familiar with sophisticated equipment such as electron microscopes, computers, thermal cyclers, and a wide variety of other equipment.

Materials Tips
Materials two 250-mL beakers, distilled water, table salt, carrot sticks, thread or string

For best results, precut carrots into equal-sized sticks. You may also wish to have students perform this activity using salt solutions of varying concentrations. If 250-mL beakers are not available, have students measure 125 mL of water into two other containers.

Safety Tips
Instruct students to discard carrot sticks after use and not eat them.

Teaching Strategies
- After students have read the opening paragraph, discuss the observations about salad vegetables and have students describe their own experiences.
- Prior to the activity, ask students to use their understanding of diffusion to explain the osmosis of water from houseplants and salads.

- Be sure students understand what it means to say that cells are in an isotonic, a hypotonic, or a hypertonic solution. Point out that distilled water is used in the activity because carrot cells are probably isotonic to tap water.

Answers to Student Worksheet

Table 1

Condition of Carrot Stick	Type of Water
Loose thread	salt water
Cells gained water	distilled water
Soft texture	salt water
Tight thread	distilled water
Firm texture	distilled water
Cells lost water	salt water

Analyze and Conclude

1. The diameter of the carrot stick indicates whether the carrot cells lost or gained water.

2. Student drawings and explanations should indicate that carrot cells will lose water and shrink when placed in salt water because salt water is hypertonic, that is, there is a greater concentration of solute molecules outside the carrot cells than within. Therefore, water diffuses out of the cells. When carrot cells are placed in the hypotonic distilled water, they will gain water because the concentration of solute molecules is lower outside the cells than within.

3. Covering fruits and vegetables with plastic wrap ensures that a relatively isotonic environment surrounds the fruit or vegetable. Therefore, water tends not to be gained or lost by cells.

4. Spraying vegetables with water keeps them fresh and crisp because the cells will not lose water when coated with an isotonic solution, such as water.

Reinforcement and Study Guide
Page 85 • Section 8.1

1. hypotonic solution
2. isotonic solution
3. hypotonic solution, hypertonic solution
4. hypertonic solution
5. h
6. a
7. c
8. d
9. f
10. b
11. e
12. g

Page 86 • Section 8.2

1. true
2. slow
3. true
4. faster
5. eight, eight
6. cell division
7. identical
8. nucleus
9. vanish
10. chromosomes
11. genetic material
12. chromatin
13. packed
14. interphase
15. mitosis
16. mitosis
17. interphase
18. interphase
19. interphase
20. mitosis
21. interphase
22. prophase
23. metaphase
24. anaphase
25. telophase
26. centrioles
27. sister chromatids
28. centromere
29. spindle fibres
30. In multicellular organisms, mitosis produces groups of cells that work together to perform a function. These groups are tissues. The tissues are organized in different combinations to form organs that have different functions.

Page 88 • Section 8.3

1. Enzymes are needed to begin and drive the cell cycle. They also direct the phases of the cell cycle.

2. Genes, segments of DNA located on the chromosomes, direct the production of these enzymes.

3. Lack of the enzymes needed to control the cell cycle, overproduction of those enzymes, or production of other enzymes at the wrong time all can cause the cell cycle to become uncontrolled.

4. Uncontrolled cell division and possibly cancer can result.

5. Certain environmental factors, such as cigarette smoke, pollution, and UV rays, can damage the genes that control the production of enzymes involved in the cell cycle. Uncontrolled cell division that leads to cancer may result.

6. A tumor is a mass of tissue that deprives normal cells of nutrients. In the final stages of cancer, cancer cells metastasize to other parts of the body, forming new tumors that disrupt organ functions.

7. Lung, colon, breast, and prostate cancers are the most prevalent.

Refuerzo y Guía de estudio
Página 89 • Sección 8.1

1. solución hipotónica
2. solución isotónica
3. solución hipotónica; solución hipertónica
4. solución hipertónica
5. h
6. a
7. c
8. d
9. f
10. b
11. e
12. g

Página 90 • Sección 8.2

1. verdadero
2. lentamente
3. verdadero
4. rápido
5. ocho, ocho
6. división celular
7. idénticas
8. núcleo
9. desvanecerse
10. cromosomas
11. material genético
12. cromatina
13. condensa
14. interfase
15. mitosis
16. mitosis
17. interfase
18. interfase
19. interfase
20. mitosis
21. interfase
22. profase
23. metafase
24. anafase
25. telofase
26. centriolos
27. cromátides hermanas
28. centrómero
29. fibras del huso
30. En los organismos multicelulares se producen mediante mitosis grupos de células que colaboran para realizar una función. Estos grupos de células forman tejidos. Los tejidos están organizados de diferentes maneras para formar órganos que llevan a cabo diferentes funciones.

Página 92 • Sección 8.3

1. Las enzimas inician y estimulan el ciclo celular, además de dirigen sus fases.

2. Los genes, segmentos de DNA localizados en los cromosomas, controlan la producción de estas enzimas.

3. La falta de las enzimas que se requieren para controlar el ciclo celular, la producción excesiva de estas enzimas o la producción de enzimas a destiempo pueden causar la pérdida de control del ciclo celular.

4. Puede ocasionar división celular descontrolada y quizá pueda producir un cáncer.

5. Ciertos factores ambientales como el humo del cigarrillo, la contaminación y los rayos UV pueden causar daños a los genes que dirigen la producción de las enzimas que controlan el ciclo celular. La división descontrolada de las células puede causar cáncer.

6. Un tumor es una masa de tejido que consume nutrientes destinados para las células sanas. En las etapas finales de un cáncer, ocurre la metástasis de las células cancerígenas y éstas se desplazan hacia otras partes del cuerpo, formando nuevos tumores que afectan las funciones de otros órganos.

7. Los tipos de cáncer de mayor incidencia son el cáncer del pulmón, del colon, de la mama y de la próstata.

Teacher Guide & Answers

Concept Map
Page 93 • *Transport Through Membranes*

1. energy
2. lower concentration
3. higher concentration
4. passive
5. simple diffusion
6. facilitated diffusion
7. osmosis
8. higher concentration
9. lower concentration

Critical Thinking
Page 94 • *Linking a Tumor Suppressor Gene to the Cell Cycle*

1. The study was done on only a few families, so conclusions about the gene's connection to cancer in the general population could not be made. Also, since the research connected the gene defect with only a rare type of breast cancer, conclusions about its involvement in more common forms of breast cancer could not be made.
2. The gene could be a part of the process of correcting mutations or a mistake in DNA replication by giving the cell time to find and correct the problem before cell division takes place. Otherwise, damaged genetic material would be passed on to daughter cells, which might lead to development of cancer or other diseases.
3. It reveals how p53 acts to prevent cells from dividing. If a cell remains in interphase, it does not go through mitosis, which leads to cell division.
4. The researchers hypothesized that one or more genes in the older DNA coded for a substance that inhibits cell division and that this substance would slow or stop division of the young cells.
5. Control of cell division involves more than two genes. More research on the genetic control of the cell cycle will be needed before the issue is completely understood.

Section Focus Transparency 18
Page 95 • *Water in the Cell*

Purpose
- To introduce the concept of osmosis

Teaching Suggestions
- Project the transparency, and have students note the difference between the two plants. Ask students to suggest why the plant in Figure B has wilted. Students most likely will suggest that the cause is a lack of water.
- Review with students the role of the plasma membrane in the cell. Tell students that one of the materials that moves freely in both directions through the plasma membrane is water. Point out that the plasma membrane determines which materials can pass through it, but that it does not determine the direction of movement for some materials, such as water. Explain that other factors help determine the direction of movement. Tell students that they will learn about these factors in this section.
- *Answers to questions on the transparency include:*

  1. In Figure A, the cytoplasm and plasma membrane reach to the cell wall. In Figure B, the cytoplasm and plasma membrane have shrunk away from the cell wall.
  2. The plant in Figure A is turgid; the plant in Figure B is wilted.

Section Focus Transparency 19
Page 96 • *Diffusion and Cell Size*

Purpose
- To introduce the concept that diffusion limits cell size

Teaching Suggestions
- Before projecting the transparency, explain to students the roles of oxygen, glucose, and carbon dioxide in a cell. (Oxygen is used in the process that breaks down glucose and releases energy, which produces carbon dioxide as a waste product.)
- Project the transparency, and have students observe the differences in the concentration of each type of molecule inside and outside the cell in Figure A. Then ask students to explain the movements of the molecules in Figure B. (Glucose and oxygen are diffusing into the cell because their concentrations are higher outside the cell than inside the cell. Carbon dioxide is diffusing out of the cell because its concentration is higher inside the cell than outside the cell.)
- *Answers to questions on the transparency include:*

  1. Oxygen, glucose, and carbon dioxide diffuse through the cell.
  2. If a cell becomes too large, materials might not be able to diffuse into and out of the cell fast enough for the cell to function properly.

Teacher Guide & Answers

Section Focus Transparency 20
Page 97 • Uncontrolled Cell Division

Purpose
- To introduce the effects of uncontrolled cell division

Teaching Suggestions
- Project the transparency, and direct attention to the large number of weeds in the garden. Discuss with students how gardeners control weed growth, for example, by picking the weeds or using herbicides.
- Have students use the analogy of the garden to explain why it might be difficult to control cancer cells without harming normal cells. (Just as an herbicide applied to a garden might kill desired plants as well as weeds, chemicals used to kill cancer cells could also harm normal cells.)
- *Answers to questions on the transparency include:*
  1. The weeds could crowd out the other plants. The weeds use nutrients and water that the other plants need, causing the other plants to die or to grow improperly.
  2. Like the weeds, the rapidly reproducing cells could crowd out the normal cells, thereby killing them.

Basic Concepts Transparency 8
Page 99 • Osmosis

Purpose
- To compare and contrast the movement of water into and out of cells under varying conditions

Teaching Suggestions
- Project the transparency and use the top half of the illustration to discuss the characteristics of a selectively permeable membrane. Then use the bottom half of the illustration to discuss the effects of isotonic, hypotonic, and hypertonic solutions on cells.
- Make certain that students realize that osmosis involves only the diffusion of water molecules, not of ions or other dissolved substances.
- Relate osmosis to homeostasis, pointing out that cells and organisms function normally only when body and cell fluids are at certain narrowly limited concentrations.

Extension: Demonstration
- Show slides of red blood cells in hypotonic, hypertonic, and isotonic solutions. (The slides can be purchased from a biological supply company.) Students will be able to see changes in the cells as a result of osmosis.

Answers to Student Worksheet

1. Water diffused across the selectively permeable membrane from left to right because the solution on the right of the membrane had a lower concentration of water. The sugar molecules did not diffuse because they are too large to pass through the membrane.
2. Like the membrane in the tube, a plasma membrane allows water molecules to pass through freely, but prevents the flow of sugar molecules through the membrane.
3. An isotonic solution has the same concentration of water and dissolved substances as found inside a cell. Therefore, water molecules randomly move into and out of the cell, but there is no net movement.
4. Osmosis does not occur since there is no net movement of water.
5. When a cell is placed in a hypotonic solution, the concentration of water inside the cell is lower than in the surrounding solution. Therefore, water diffuses into the cell.
6. The pressure decreases as water diffuses out of the cell.
7. Animal cells can burst in a hypotonic solution if their plasma membrane is unable to withstand the increasing pressure inside the cell due to the movement of water into the cell.
8. In the absence of water or when placed in a hypertonic environment, plant cells lose water. As a result, the plasma membrane and cytoplasm shrink away from the cell wall. The cells lose some of their internal pressure and their shape, and the plant wilts.

Basic Concepts Transparency 9
Page 101 • Active Transport

Purpose
- To show the process of active transport

Teaching Suggestions
- Project the transparency and have students follow the movement of the ion from one side of the plasma membrane to the opposite side. Point out the changes in the shape of the carrier protein, which allows the ion to move through the plasma membrane.
- Have students compare endocytosis and exocytosis. Point out that exocytosis is a vital process in the body's utilization of hormones, which are manufactured by cells but cannot leave them via passive transport.

Extension: Research

- Have students research the sodium-potassium pump, which is an active transport system that allows nerve cells to send impulses. Students can draw a diagram similar to the one shown in the transparency to explain how the sodium-potassium pump works.

Answers to Student Worksheet

1. carrier protein
2. The ions are more concentrated on one side of the plasma membrane than on the other side.
3. Cells must use energy in order to counteract the tendency of particles to diffuse from a region of higher concentration to a region of lower concentration.
4. A carrier protein binds with an ion or other particle to be transported against the concentration gradient. Using chemical energy from the cell, the protein then changes shape in order to carry the particle through the plasma membrane to the other side. When the particle is released, the protein reverts to its original shape.
5. The energy is produced by chemical reactions in the mitochondria of the cell.
6. In endocytosis, a particle is not taken through the plasma membrane. Rather, the plasma membrane engulfs the particle and makes a sac or vacuole around it. That portion of the membrane then breaks away, bringing the vacuole and its contents into the cell.
7. Endocytosis is classified as active transport because it requires energy.
8. Exocytosis; in exocytosis, materials are expelled from a vacuole.

Basic Concepts Transparency 10
Page 103 • Mitosis

Purpose
- To review the phases and importance of mitosis

Teaching Suggestions
- Project the transparency. Discuss the processes and structures involved in each phase of mitosis.
- Point out that although four phases of mitosis are illustrated separately, the process is continuous, with each phase gradually developing into the next.

Extension: Photography
- Interested students might wish to take microphotographs of cells in various phases of mitosis. If your school does not have the necessary equipment, try enlisting the help of a local college or university.

Answers to Student Worksheet

1. The spindle forms during prophase. As the two centriole pairs move to opposite ends of the cell, the spindle forms between them.
2. metaphase
3. prophase
4. Cytokinesis follows mitosis.
5. The cells are those of animals since they contain centrioles, which are not present in plant cells.
6. Cytokinesis is the division of the cytoplasm of daughter cells, which occurs after mitosis. During cytokinesis in animal cells, the plasma membrane pinches in along the equator until two separate cells are formed. In plant cells, the cytoplasm is divided by the formation of a cell plate across the equator. A new cell wall is then secreted on each side of the cell plate until the two new cells are separate.
7. It ensures genetic continuity and the continuation of cellular processes vital to the survival of the organism.

Reteaching Skills Transparency 11
Page 105 • Active Versus Passive Transport

Purpose
- To demonstrate the similarities and differences between active transport and passive transport
- Skill: Comparing and contrasting

Teaching Suggestions
- Present the transparency. Ask students to make a table that compares passive transport and active transport with respect to concentration gradient, use of transport proteins, and energy usage.

Extension: Collection
- For the next several days, have the class create a "rolling collection" of examples of ways that concentration gradients function in their lives—"rolling" because students add items over the coming days as they learn more about biology. Items can include essays, drawings, sculptures, and other displays. Examples may come only from biology or from biology and other aspects of students' lives.

Answers to Student Worksheet

1. The statement is accurate because molecules move from areas of higher concentration to areas of lower concentration. It is not accurate because it implies that by the end of the process all the molecules have moved to a new place. In reality, the

result of diffusion is an even distribution of molecules throughout the area.

2. *Concentration gradient* is the difference in concentration of a substance across space.

3. The arrow in A should show molecules moving from right to left, from the higher concentration (inside the cell) to the lower concentration (outside the cell).

4. The arrow in B should show molecules moving from left to right, from the lower concentration (outside the cell) to the higher concentration (inside the cell).

5. The transparency illustrates facilitated diffusion because it shows the use of transport proteins.

6. During passive transport, the cell uses no energy to move the particles.

7. Energy is needed because the particles are moving against the concentration gradient from an area of lower concentration to an area of higher concentration.

8. Carrier proteins bind with ions or molecules near the plasma membrane. As they do so, the proteins change shape. Then, using energy, the carrier proteins move the particles to the other side of the membrane.

Reteaching Skills Transparency 12
Page 107 • Osmosis and Hypotonic, Hypertonic, and Isotonic Solutions

Purpose
- To differentiate between hypotonic, hypertonic, and isotonic solutions and compare the movement of water molecules in cells placed in each solution
- Skills: Observing and inferring, using numbers

Teaching Suggestions
- Present the transparency and, for each illustration, have students find the approximate ratio of water molecules to dissolved particles both inside and outside the cell. Emphasize that students should calculate the ratios, not simply count the number of molecules on either side of the membrane. Have students record the ratios they calculated.
- Use the overlay to correct or verify students' calculations.
- Discuss what will happen to the cell in each drawing. In the hypotonic solution, water molecules will move into the cell by osmosis; in the hypertonic solution, water molecules will move out of the cell by osmosis;

and in the isotonic solution, water molecules will move into and out of the cell at the same rate.

Extension: Demonstration
- Demonstrate the process of osmosis by soaking a wilted lettuce leaf in water overnight. Ask students to explain their observations.

Answers to Student Worksheet
1. a. Osmosis is the diffusion of water molecules through a selectively permeable membrane.
   b. In a hypotonic solution, the concentration of dissolved substances outside the cell is lower than the concentration inside the cell.
   c. In a hypertonic solution, the concentration of dissolved substances outside the cell is higher than the concentration inside the cell.
   d. In an isotonic solution, the concentration of dissolved substances is the same outside the cell and inside the cell.
2. Water molecules will move into the cell by osmosis.
3. Water molecules will move out of the cell by osmosis.
4. Water molecules will move in and out of the cell at random.
5. In a hypotonic condition, a plant will be rigid—water will diffuse into the cells, increasing pressure inside the cells and causing the cells to fill the cell walls completely. In a hypertonic condition, a plant will wilt—water will diffuse out of the cells, decreasing pressure inside the cells and causing the cells to pull away from the cell walls.
6. Unlike osmosis, facilitated diffusion occurs with the help of transport proteins in the plasma membrane.

Reteaching Skills Transparency 13
Page 109 • Cell Cycle

Purpose
- To delineate the life cycle of a cell
- Skill: Concept mapping

Teaching Suggestions
- Present the transparency. Discuss the activities that occur during interphase. Point out that in multicellular organisms, interphase is the time when cells perform their specialized function, such as producing hormones or secreting gastric juices for digestion. Also during this period, the centrioles and chromosomes replicate in preparation for mitosis.

Teacher Guide & Answers

- Then discuss the phases of mitosis. Point out that cytokinesis, not shown on the transparency, occurs after mitosis. Some cells, such as skeletal muscles, do not always go through cytokinesis. As a result, these cells have more than one nucleus.

- Tell students that the cell cycles can vary in length. For example, cells of the immune system divide rapidly when the body encounters a foreign substance and divide slowly during other periods.

Extension: Role Play

- Mitosis can be a difficult concept for students. This demonstration will enable them to "see" the process in concrete terms. Divide students into groups of about 8–10 students each. Then divide the students into pairs. Three of the pairs represent replicated chromosomes, so they are given stick-on labels on which are written 1-A, 1-B, 2-A, 2-B, 3-A, and 3-B. Draw a chalk circle on the floor. Have all the A's move into the circle to represent the unreplicated chromosomes. The B's enter the circle when DNA is synthesized. The "non-chromosome" students then direct the others in their actions (when to move as a pair, when to separate, where to go, etc.), as they move through the cell cycle. Repeat the process at least twice, changing roles so that all members play an active role.

Answers to Student Worksheet

1. Diffusion is a slow process. If a cell becomes too large, substances may take too long to reach the cell's organelles, which may cause the cell to die.

2. If a cell becomes too large, it may not have enough DNA to produce all the proteins it needs.

3. As a cell's size increases, its volume increases much faster than its surface area. As a result, the cell would need to take in nutrients and excrete wastes faster than the available surface area would allow. Eventually, the cell would starve and/or be poisoned.

4. Interphase: The cell grows; the chromosomes and centrioles duplicate; organelles are made in preparation for mitosis.

5. Prophase: The chromatin coils into visible chromosomes; nuclear envelope and nucleolus disappear; a spindle forms between the centrioles, which have moved to the opposite ends of the cell.

6. Metaphase: The chromosomes move to the equator of the spindle; each chromatid is attached to a separate spindle fiber by its centromere.

7. Anaphase: The centromeres split; sister chromatids are pulled apart to opposite poles of the cell.

8. Telophase: The nucleolus and nuclear envelope reappear; the chromosomes begin to uncoil; two new cells form.

Chapter Assessment
Page 111 • *Reviewing Vocabulary*

1. active transport
2. anaphase
3. hypotonic
4. cell cycle
5. interphase
6. gene
7. metaphase
8. sister chromatids
9. cancer
10. facilitated diffusion
11. mitosis
12. endocytosis
13. centromeres
14. During prophase, the spindle forms between the pairs of centrioles.
15. Organs are made of tissues organized in various combinations.

Page 112 • *Understanding Main Ideas (Part A)*

1. c	6. d
2. a	7. c
3. b	8. c
4. b	9. b
5. d	10. d

Page 113 • *Understanding Main Ideas (Part B)*

1. C
2. prophase
3. centriole
4. spindle
5. D
6. A separate nuclear envelope is forming around each set of chromosomes. The spindle is breaking down.
7. D, A, F, C, E, B   or   A, F, C, E, B, D
8. During cytokinesis in animal cells, the plasma membrane pinches in along the equator to form two new cells. In plant cells, a cell plate forms across the equator; then a plasma membrane forms around each new cell and a new cell wall is secreted on each side of the cell plate.

Page 114 • *Thinking Critically*

1. higher
2. Na^+
3. Ca^{2+}
4. 30 mM
5. yes; Na^+ ions
6. To maintain different concentrations of ions on either side of the plasma membrane, the cell must move the ions against a concentration gradient. To do so, the cell uses active transport, in which carrier proteins bind with the ions and move them across the membrane. This process requires energy.

Page 115 • *Applying Scientific Methods*

1. Colchicine causes cells to produce multiple sets of chromosomes in their nuclei.
2. The untreated root tips were the control group; the root tips treated with colchicine were the experimental group.
3. treatment of the onion roots with colchicine
4. the cell cycle of the onion root cells
5. Answers may vary. The slides of untreated root tips will show cells in interphase and in various stages of mitosis. The slides of treated root tips will show cells only in interphase and in prophase. The cells in prophase will have no spindle fibers, and they may show some cells with multiple sets of chromosomes.
6. The colchicine stopped mitosis after prophase.
7. If the cells of the colchicine-treated onion root and the cells of the untreated onion root appeared in the same stages of mitosis under the microscope, the researcher could conclude that the colchicine had no effect.
8. It states the problem; a conclusion is never stated as a question.
9. The researcher might first investigate the structure of spindle fibers and the chemical constituents of colchicine and then design an experiment that specifically tests how colchicine blocks the formation of spindle fibers.
10. When a plant has extra sets of chromosomes, it has extra copies of genes, which produce more of the proteins that the genes code for. Proteins are used in cellular reactions and in cellular structures. Having the additional proteins causes the fruits and flowers to be larger.

Student Recording Sheet
Page 117

Answers can be found on page 218 in the Teacher Wraparound Edition.

Chapter 9

MiniLab 9.1
Page 120 • Separating Pigments

Expected Results

As the solvent (rubbing alcohol) moves up the filter paper, slight differences in color will begin to appear, starting with green and progressing to yellow and perhaps orange.

Analysis

1. Students may indicate that the solvent moved up the filter paper about 5 cm and then stopped. As the solvent progressed, varying shades of green and yellow appeared.

2. Different components of the plant solution have varying attraction for the filter paper. Therefore the colors will be deposited at different distances up the filter paper.

MiniLab 9.2
Page 121 • Use Isotopes to Understad Photosynthesis

Expected Results

Student models will show that all carbon from carbon dioxide ends up in CH_2O; all oxygen from carbon dioxide ends up in CH_2O and water; all hydrogen from water (on the left side) ends up in CH_2O and water.

Analysis

1. If an isotope is radioactive, it can be traced by identifying the radioactive product of the reaction.

2. a. incorporated into CH_2O or water
   b. incorporated into CH_2O
   c. incorporated into CH_2O and water

MiniLab 9.3
Page 122 • Determine if Apple Juice Ferments

Analysis

1. CO_2
2. The rate would increase.
3. Warm water increases the metabolic rate of the yeast.
4. Anaerobic, because no oxygen is available in the bulb of the pipette covered with water.

Internet BioLab
Page 123 • What factors influence photosynthesis?

Sample Data

Data Table

	Control	Color 1	Color 2
Bubbles observed in five minutes	Results will vary, but will yield the highest number.	Results will vary depending on color of cellophane.	Results will vary depending on color of cellophane.

Analyze and Conclude

1. The bubbles emerged from the end of the stem of the *Elodea* plant.

2. Oxygen is an end product of photosynthesis. As the rate of photosynthesis changes, so will the rate at which oxygen is produced.

3. The rate for the control setup should be the greatest and therefore the highest line. The rates corresponding to colored, filtered light will be lower than the control. Results will vary depending on the color of the cellophane the students use.

4. Sodium hydrogen carbonate is a source of carbon dioxide. If you change the amount of sodium hydrogen carbonate, it will change the amount of carbon dioxide available to the aquatic plants. This variable change may affect the rate of photosynthesis.

Real World BioApplications
Page 125 • Bioluminescence and Behavior

Planning the Activity

Use this activity with Chapter 9 of the text, after students have been introduced to the relationship between stored energy, ATP, and ADP.

Purpose

Students evaluate information from a series of experiments and draw conclusions about the nature and uses of bioluminescence. The activity gives students an opportunity to employ critical thinking skills as they draw conclusions based on research data.

Career Applications

The critical thinking skills reinforced in this activity are directly related to the skills used in biochemistry. Biochemical technicians often assist biochemists in the study of the chemical composition of living things. The goal is to understand the complex chemical combinations and reactions involved in metabolism, reproduction, growth, and heredity. Successful biomedical technicians are likely to be graduates of science techni-cian training programs or applied science technology programs and are well-trained on equipment used in laboratories and production facilities.

Teaching Suggestions

- After students have read the introduction, review the role of ATP in storing chemical energy in a cell.

- Ask students what form of energy characterizes bio-luminescence (light). Invite students to discuss how a cell, or an organism, might change chemical energy to light energy.

- It may be useful to review how to formulate a hypothesis to answer a question or solve a problem. Students will be designing experiments to explain the use of bioluminescence by a marine organism in Part B. Students will not be expected to carry out their experiments.

Answers to Student Worksheet

Part A

1. Luciferin, luciferase, and oxygen are needed for bioluminescence.
2. The different chemical compositions of luciferin and luciferase may be responsible for the different colors of light produced.
3. The amount of light produced increases in direct proportion to the amount of ATP present.
4. luciferin + <u>luciferase</u> + <u>oxygen</u> + <u>ATP</u> = oxidized luciferin + AMP (adenosine monophos-phate) + PP (pyrophosphate) + water + light

Part B

1. Students' hypotheses may vary but should be clearly stated in an *if/then* format. Hypotheses should also reflect an understanding of controls and dependent and independent variables.
2. Students' responses may vary but should indicate an understanding of what variables should be changed in order to test their hypotheses.
3. Students' experimental procedures may vary but should reflect a reasonable step-by-step sequence for collecting and recording data. Procedures should also indicate which experimental condi-tions must be controlled, what will constitute the control and experimental groups, which are the dependent and independent variables, and what results are needed to confirm the hypothesis.

Reinforcement and Study Guide
Page 127 • Section 9.1

1. work
2. ATP
3. energy
4. chemical bonds
5. adenine
6. ribose
7. charged
8. phosphate
9. Energy that is used to add a phosphate group to ADP becomes stored as a chemical bond in the resulting ATP molecule. The stored energy is released when ATP is broken down to ADP and a phosphate group.
10. Answers may vary. Cells use energy to make new molecules, maintain homeostasis, transmit nerve impulses, move, and produce light.

Page 128 • Section 9.2

1. true
2. light-dependent
3. oxygen
4. chloroplasts
5. true
6. 4
7. 3
8. 1
9. 6
10. 2
11. 5
12. The electrons are replaced by the splitting of water molecules during photosynthesis.
13. Oxygen, as well as hydrogen ions, is produced when water molecules are split during photosynthesis.
14. c
15. b
16. c
17. b
18. d
19. a
20. a
21. b
22. c
23. d

Page 130 • Section 9.3

1. glucose
2. 2ADP
3. 2PGAL
4. 4ATP
5. 2 pyruvic acid
6. 2NADH + 2H$^+$
7. Pyruvic acid combines with coenzyme A to form acetyl-CoA.
8. The electrons are passed through an electron transport chain, releasing energy at each step.
9. citric acid cycle and electron transport chain
10. Oxygen is the final electron acceptor in the electron transport chain.
11. Fermentation occurs when no oxygen is available. Fermentation produces fewer ATP molecules.
12. In cellular respiration, chemical energy is released, whereas in photosynthesis, chemical energy is stored. Products of cellular respiration, CO_2 and H_2O, are used in photosynthesis. Products of photosynthesis, glucose and O_2, are used in cellular respiration.

Refuerzo y Guía de estudio
Página 131 • Sección 9.1

1. funciones biológicas
2. ATP
3. energía
4. enlaces químicos
5. adenosina
6. ribosa
7. cargadas
8. fosfato
9. La energía que se usa para añadir un grupo fosfato al ADP y convertirlo en una molécula de ATP, queda almacenada en el enlace químico. La energía almacenada se libera cuando el ATP se desdobla en ADP y un grupo fosfato.
10. Las respuestas variarán. La célula usa la energía para fabricar nuevas moléculas, para mantener la homeostasis, para transmitir impulsos nerviosos, para moverse y para producir luz.

Página 132 • Sección 9.2

1. verdadero
2. independiente de la luz
3. oxígeno
4. del cloroplasto

5. verdadero
6. 4
7. 3
8. 1
9. 6
10. 2
11. 5
12. Los electrones son reemplazados por el rompimiento de moléculas de agua durante la fotosíntesis.
13. Cuando se rompen las moléculas de agua durante la fotosíntesis se producen oxígeno y iones de hidrógeno.
14. c
15. b
16. c
17. b
18. d
19. a
20. a
21. b
22. c
23. d

Página 134 • Sección 9.3

1. glucosa
2. 2ADP
3. 2PGAL
4. 4ATP
5. 2 ácido pirúvico
6. NADH + 2H$^+$
7. El ácido pirúvico se combina con la coenzima A para formar acetil-CoA.
8. Los electrones pasan a través de una cadena de transporte electrónico, liberando energía en cada paso.
9. Durante el ciclo del ácido cítrico y en la cadena de transporte electrónico.
10. El oxígeno es el aceptor final en la cadena de transporte electrónico.
11. La fermentación ocurre cuando no hay oxígeno disponible. La fermentación produce menos moléculas de ATP.
12. Durante la respiración celular se libera energía química, mientras que durante la fotosíntesis se almacena energía química. Los productos de la respiración celular, CO_2 y H_2O, se usan en la fotosíntesis. Los productos de la fotosíntesis, glucosa y O_2, se usan durante la respiración celular.

Concept Mapping
*Page 135 • Photosynthesis: Trapping the
Sun's Energy*

1. cholroplasts
2. stroma
3. chlorophyll
4. sunlight
5. water
6. carbon dioxide
7. energy
8. oxygen
9. hydrogen ions
10. light-dependent reactions
11. chemical energy
12. glucose

Problem Solving
*Page 136 • Two Factors Affecting
Photosynthesis*

1. The rate of photosynthesis increases as light intensity increases to about 9000 lumens, indicating that there are other factors that limit photosynthesis.
2. The rate of photosynthesis does not increase; it levels off.
3. Accept reasonable answers. A plant could carry on photosynthesis and survive in very intense light.
4. The rate of photosynthesis increases as the temperature increases to about 33°C.
5. The rate of photosynthesis sharply decreases.
6. Accept reasonable answers. The increasing temperature causes enzymes to break down, which results in a rapid decrease in the rate of photosynthesis.
7. Light intensity of 9000 lumens and a temperature of about 33°C allow the highest photosynthesis rate.

Section Focus Transparency 21
Page 137 • Using Energy

Purpose
- To illustrate that all organisms use energy for a variety of tasks

Teaching Suggestions
- Project the transparency, and have students identify the various living organisms and the activities of each.

- Review with students the cell structures they learned about in Chapter 7, such as the mitochondria, plasma membrane, and Golgi apparatus. Remind students that these structures need energy to carry out their functions.
- *Answers to questions on the transparency include:*

1. Answers will vary, but might include that all organisms in the picture are using energy to grow and maintain homeostasis. The animals are also using energy to move.
2. Answers will vary, but might include that organisms use energy to reproduce, develop, and repair body tissue.

Section Focus Transparency 22
Page 138 • Photosynthesis

Purpose
- To illustrate that light is necessary for photosynthesis to occur

Teaching Suggestions
- Project the transparency, and direct students' attention to the two experimental setups and the differences between them. Students should observe that the test tube in Setup A is in the dark covered with a box. The test tube in Setup B is exposed to light.
- Have students recall dependent and independent variables from Chapter 1. Tell students that oxygen gas is a product of photosynthesis. Ask students to identify the independent variable (light) and dependent variable (gas production) in this experiment.
- *Answers to questions on the transparency include:*

1. The test tube in Setup A shows that almost no gas has been produced over time. The test tube in Setup B shows that a large quantity of gas has been produced.
2. The results indicate that light is necessary for photosynthesis to occur.

Section Focus Transparency 23
Page 139 • Cellular Respiration

Purpose
- To introduce the process of cellular respiration

Teaching Suggestions
- Project the transparency, and direct students' attention to each of the organisms shown. Some students

might not be familiar with the paramecium. Explain that the paramecium is a unicellular organism that feeds primarily on bacteria.

- Point out to students that the food these organisms use contains energy, but that the energy must be released before cells can use it. Explain that the process by which food molecules are broken down to release energy is called cellular respiration, and that students will learn more about this process in this section.

- *Answers to questions on the transparency include:*

  1. All three organisms require energy.
  2. The paramecium and the grasshopper get energy from the food they consume. The tree uses the energy in sunlight to produce food during photosynthesis.

Basic Concepts Transparency 11
Page 141 • ATP–ADP Cycle

Purpose

- To show the reactions by which energy is made available to cells

Teaching Suggestions

- Explain that the ATP–ADP cycle can proceed only if certain raw materials are present. These include phosphates and high-energy molecules, both of which are obtained from foods. High-energy molecules, such as sugars (including glucose), fats, and starches, are the source of energy that is used by the cell to make ATP.

- Point out that because glucose is produced by photosynthesis and glucose is the molecule used by cells to obtain energy for the conversion of ADP to ATP, the primary source of energy for almost all living things is the sun.

- Identify dietary sources of phosphates and glucose. Phosphates are abundant in dairy products, whereas fruits and vegetables are rich in sugars and starches that the body breaks down into glucose. Fats are converted to glycogen, another source of glucose.

Extension: Poster

- Organize students into work groups. Have each group construct a poster, using illustrations and text, to describe the uses of cell energy and to highlight the role of ATP–ADP conversion reactions in those uses.

Answers to Student Worksheet

1. ATP contains three phosphate groups, whereas ADP contains two phosphate groups.
2. adenine, ribose, and phosphate
3. More energy is stored in ATP. Energy is stored in the bonds that link one phosphate group to another.
4. A phosphate group combines with ADP. This process requires an input of energy, which is stored in the new phosphate bond that forms to make ATP. Water is a by-product of this reaction.
5. Water is used to remove a phosphate group from ATP. As the phosphate group is removed, energy stored in the bond that linked it to its neighbor phosphate group is released.
6. Each reaction forms products that are used in the other reaction. In one reaction, water is used to convert ATP to ADP with the release of a phosphate group and energy. In the other reaction, ADP, a phosphate group, and energy are used to produce ATP and water. The ATP can then be converted back into ADP and the cycle repeats again.
7. To release the energy stored in ATP, proteins bind ATP. When the phosphate group is released from the ATP, the protein releases the ADP that is formed and then binds with another ATP.
8. Answers include to make new molecules move, send nerve impulses, and maintain homeostasis. Accept all reasonable answers.

Basic Concepts Transparency 12
Page 143 • Photosynthesis

Purpose

- To distinguish between the light-dependent reactions and the light-independent reactions of photosynthesis

Teaching Suggestions

- Project the base transparency and point out that both the light-dependent reactions and the light-independent reactions make up the process of photosynthesis. Ask students to explain what is happening at points A, B, and C on the transparency. Then display the overlay and compare students' responses with the information given on the overlay.

- Point out that in the light-dependent reactions, energy is released by electrons in a series of

Teacher Guide & Answers

controlled steps, known as the electron transport chain. Thus, the illustration of the light-dependent reactions in the transparency should be considered a simplification of a very complex, multi-step process.

- Tell students that the light-independent reactions are also referred to as the Calvin cycle. Discuss how the reactions are cycles.

Extension: Research

- Have students research the various types of chlorophyll molecules and how the different types of chlorophyll are used in the light-dependent reactions. Students might also research the arrangement of chlorophyll molecules in the thylakoid membrane, referred to as photosystems I and II.

Answers to Student Worksheet

1. The electrons in chlorophyll absorb the sun's energy, leave the chlorophyll molecules, and are passed along a series of proteins embedded in the thylakoid membrane, called an electron transport chain.
2. As an electron moves down an electron transport chain, it releases some of its absorbed energy, which may be used to make ATP or to pump hydrogen ions into the thylakoid disc.
3. oxygen, hydrogen ions, and electrons; photolysis
4. The oxygen is the primary source of Earth's atmospheric oxygen.
5. ATP and NADPH
6. Carbon fixation occurs during the light-dependent reactions, when carbon dioxide from the air is used to make carbohydrates.
7. ATP and NADPH from the light-dependent reactions
8. The final product is the 6-carbon sugar glucose, which is used by cells to make sugars, starches, and cellulose.

Basic Concepts Transparency 13
Page 145 • Cellular Respiration

Purpose
- To show the process by which glucose is broken down to release energy

Teaching Suggestions
- Point out that the chemical origin of energy for cellular activity is the food molecule glucose. The energy stored in glucose is released during glycolysis and aerobic respiration and then stored in ATP. If

necessary, body cells can obtain energy from the breakdown of fats or proteins, although these processes are less efficient.

- To make the connection clear between the three processes shown in the transparency, have students pick out the substance that links one process to the next. Pyruvic acid links glycosis to aerobic respiration in the mitochondrion, while acetyl-CoA is a link to the citric acid cycle.
- Ask students to redraw the three sets of reactions to show how they are interconnected. Students should pay special attention to the roles ATP and ADP play in the connections.

Extension: Models
- Using building toys, students can build models of the molecules involved in glycolysis and aerobic respiration, rearrange them, and take them apart as would occur in each stage of the processes.

Answers to Student Worksheet

1. The energy comes from the conversion of two molecules of ATP to two molecules of ADP.
2. Glucose is broken down. Pyruvic acid is the end product.
3. The ratio of glucose molecules to the net number of ATP molecules is 1:2 because for every molecule of glucose that is split, four molecules of ATP are produced and two are used.
4. Glycolysis is anaerobic, whereas the breakdown of pyruvic acid and the citric acid cycle are aerobic.
5. The breakdown occurs in the mitochondria of a cell.
6. acetyl-CoA
7. The acetyl-CoA produced by the breakdown of pyruvic acid enters the citric acid cycle where it combines with oxaloacetic acid to form citric acid.
8. carbon dioxide
9. They both give up electrons at the electron transport chain.

Reteaching Skills Transparency 14
Page 147 • Electron Transport Chain

Purpose
- To show the overall steps by which a cell uses glucose to make ATP
- Skill: Sequencing

Teacher Guide & Answers

Teaching Suggestions

- Present the transparency. Point out that the glucose molecule travels to the cell through the bloodstream after the food that it was once a part of has been digested.
- Review with students how glucose molecules are broken down during cellular respiration.

Extension: Challenge

- Challenge students to think of processes other than the movement of electrons through an electron transport chain in which energy is lost gradually or in steps. For example, students might describe the loss of energy as it moves through a food chain or the loss of energy as a windup toy slows down.

Answers to Student Worksheet

1. A plant makes glucose by the process of photosynthesis.
2. from the food it eats
3. ATP is a molecule with three high-energy bonds that bind three phosphate groups to an adenosine molecule.
4. When one of the phosphate groups is removed from ATP, energy is released to do work within the cell. When a phosphate group is bound to ADP, energy is stored for later use in the cell.
5. If the energy in a molecule were released all at once, it could harm the cell. Releasing energy in small amounts enables the cell to store the energy in "packages" in the bonds of ATP molecules for later use.
6. in the mitochondria
7. Responses will vary. Students should include such things as writing the answer, blinking eyes, hearing sounds in the room, breathing, blood circulating, thinking, swallowing, digesting food, sweating (if the room is warm) or shivering (if the room is cold), and growing hair or fingernails. Accept all reasonable answers.

Reteaching Skills Transparency 15
Page 149 • Photosynthesis and Cellular Respiration

Purpose

- To compare and contrast photosynthesis and cellular respiration
- Skill: Sequencing

Teaching Suggestions

- Remind students that only plant cells and other photosynthetic cells contain chloroplasts. Thus, plants can produce their own food, whereas animals must obtain food by feeding on plants or on animals that eat plants.
- Then use the overlays to emphasize the interrelationships of photosynthesis and cellular respiration. Point out the cyclical nature of the two processes. Use the base transparency to discuss photosynthesis and cellular respiration. Make sure students know that plant cells and animal cells have mitochondria and that cellular respiration occurs in both types of cells.

Extension: Challenge

- Have students use library resources to make a poster that shows how a total of 38 ATP molecules are produced during cellular respiration.

Answers to Student Worksheet

1. Photosynthesis takes place in the chloroplast, and cellular respiration takes place in the mitochondrion.
2. Carbon dioxide and water move into chloroplasts and out of mitochondria; oxygen and glucose move out of chloroplasts and into mitochondria.
3. chloroplast
4. They both involve oxygen, carbon dioxide, water, high-energy compounds, and the movement of electrons in transport chains. Also, they both occur inside specific organelles.
5. Photosynthesis stores energy in glucose. Cellular respiration releases the energy stored in glucose. The two processes also have different reactants and products, and they occur in different organelles.
6. glucose
7. The Calvin cycle in chloroplasts is linked to the citric acid cycle in mitochondria by the production of carbon dioxide in the mitochondria and the utilization of carbon dioxide in the chloroplasts.
8. The equations are the reverse of each other.

Chapter Assessment
Page 151 • Reviewing Vocabulary

1. light-dependent reactions
2. photosynthesis
3. electron transport chain
4. Chlorphyll
5. photolysis

6. glycolysis
7. Calvin cycle
8. citric acid cycle
9. Aerobic processes require oxygen; anaerobic processes do not.
10. Both are complex series of reactions that involve energy, require enzymes, occur in specific organelles, and involve movement of electrons. In photosynthesis, CO_2 and H_2O are used to store energy in sugar, and oxygen is given off as a waste. In cellular respiration, energy is released when sugar is broken down in the presence of oxygen; CO_2 and H_2O are given off as wastes.

Page 152 • Understanding Main Ideas (Part A)

1. a
2. b
3. d
4. c
5. d
6. b
7. d
8. a
9. b
10. b

Page 153 • Understanding Main Ideas (Part B)

1. a. They require energy.
   b. The energy required for each activity is obtained by the breakdown of ATP to ADP and inorganic phosphate.
2. a. Both industries use yeast to produce alcohol and carbon dioxide by the process of alcoholic fermentation.
   b. The wine industry uses the alcohol to make the wine; the bread industry uses the carbon dioxide to make the bread dough rise.
3. If oxygen is present, production of acetyl-CoA, the citric acid cycle, and electron transport chain follow in order. If no oxygen is present, either lactic acid fermentation or alcoholic fermentation follows.
4. Carbon fixation occurs during the Calvin cycle, when a carbon atom from atmospheric carbon dioxide is added to a 5-carbon sugar.
5. The rate at which oxygen is supplied to the muscle cells limits the level of aerobic respiration that can occur. As a result, anaerobic lactic acid fermentation takes place, changing pyruvic acid to lactic acid. The buildup of lactic acid in the muscle cells causes muscle fatigue.

Page 154 • Thinking Critically

1. glycolysis, 2; citric acid cycle, 2; electron transport chain, 32
2. 36 molecules

3. Fermentation yields no molecules of ATP. Since glycolysis yields a net gain of 2 ATP molecules, and glycolysis combined with fermentation also yields 2 molecules of ATP, fermentation must produce zero molecules of ATP.
4. The *Elodea* in the two test tubes must have taken in the CO_2 since the solution in those test tubes changed to blue, but the solution in the control test tube remained yellow.

Page 155 • Applying Scientific Methods

1. He reasoned that the bacteria would be more numerous where more oxygen was present.
2. No; the purpose was to determine the effect of different colors of light on the rate of photosynthesis.
3. Since oxygen is a product of photosynthesis, he reasoned that more oxygen indicated a greater rate of photosynthesis.
4. He was using bacteria to determine oxygen levels. Anaerobic bacteria do not require oxygen for their life activities.
5. He would conclude that the rate of photosynthesis is greatest in violet light and orange light.
6. the different colors of light
7. Answers will vary. He could have exposed the alga and bacteria to white light and to complete darkness.
8. Yes, his hypothesis was that various colors of light affect the rate of photosynthesis differently, and he observed that they do.

Student Recording Sheet
Page 157

Answers can be found on page 242 in the Teacher Wraparound Edition.

Teacher Guide & Answers

Unit 3 BioDigest

Reinforcement and Study Guide
Page 159

1. proton
2. atom
3. molecule
4. electron
5. nucleus
6. neutron
7. membrane
8. Eukaryotic cells
9. prokaryotic cells
10. lipid bilayer
11. nucleus
12. proteins
13. endoplasmic recticulum
14. chloroplasts
15. structure
16. Flagella
17. Diffusion is the net movement of a substance from an area of higher concentration to an area of lower concentration.
18. Osmosis is the diffusion of water across a selectively permeable membrane.
19. Active transport is the movement of molecules against a concentration gradient.
20. d
21. a
22. e
23. b
24. c
25. energy
26. Light-independent
27. true
28. each molecule

Refuerzo y Guía de estudio
Página 161

1. protón
2. átomo
3. molécula
4. electrón
5. núcleo
6. neutrón
7. membrana
8. Eucariotas
9. procariotas
10. capa doble lípida
11. núcleo
12. proteínas
13. retículo endoplásmico
14. cloroplastos
15. estructura
16. Flagelos
17. La difusión es el movimiento de una sustancia desde un área de mayor concentración hacia un área de menor concentración.
18. La osmosis es la difusión de agua a través de una membrana con permeabilidad selectiva.
19. El transporte activo es el movimiento de moléculas en contra de un gradiente de concentración.
20. d
21. a
22. e
23. b
24. c
25. energía
26. fase independiente
27. verdadero
28. cada molécula

Student Recording Sheet
Page 163

Answers can be found on page 248 in the Teacher Wraparound Edition.